THE COMPLETE
MUSASHI
THE BOOK OF FIVE RINGS
AND OTHER WORKS

Translated with an Introduction by
ALEXANDER BENNETT

Foreword by **GRAHAM SAYER**

TUTTLE Publishing
Tokyo | Rutland, Vermont | Singapore

Dedicated to the memory of two modern "Sword Saints"
Ichiro Shirafuji (1945–2011) & Tadao Toda (1939–2016)

Contents

Foreword

People from all walks of life, from motivational business speakers to athletes have touched on the life and works of Miyamoto Musashi in various ways to enhance their message or achieve their goals.

As an avid practitioner of the traditional Japanese martial art of Kendo, the late Victor Harris translation of Miyamoto Musashi's *Gorin-no-sho* (The Book of Five Rings) was the first book I read seriously with the hope it would have some bearing on the way I think about and shape my Kendo journey.

In 1988, I was lucky enough to spend an evening with the late Mr. Harris, who convinced me that I needed to read *Gorin-no-sho* at least once every two to three years in order to gain a greater understanding of the underpinning philosophy as my technical abilities progressed.

The wisdom contained in *Gorin-no-sho* is too profound to summarize in a few short paragraphs, but allow me to present three lessons that I have attempted to apply to my Kendo over the years:

1. Never take any opponent lightly, regardless of their rank.
(Earth Scroll)
2. Strive to focus on decisive strikes rather than hits.
(Water Scroll)
3. "Stopping the Start," the teaching in which you snuff out your opponent's opportunity to attack.
(Fire Scroll)

All of these lessons are paramount to the study of Kendo and other martial arts, and indeed provide valuable lessons for life itself.

Countless novels and movies that have been produced about this celebrated swordsman have been the main source of information for aficionados of Japanese culture to catch a glimpse of Miyamoto Musashi's life and career. Unfortunately, portrayals in popular culture are inevitably more fiction than fact. Thanks to this publication, however, readers will be able to tap into the centuries-old knowledge of arguably Japan's greatest swordsman with confidence of its authenticity.

If you are a martial arts practitioner, nothing could be so welcome. Even if you have no interest in the martial arts or Japanese history, you will be sure to find by reading between the lines, a kind of universal wisdom that can be applied to all facets of your everyday life, relationships, and work.

Dr. Bennett has combined his many years as a scholar of Japanese history with his immense experience and background in ancient fighting arts to produce this magnificent translation of Musashi's works. His ability to open this world up to non-Japanese and Japanese readers alike is unparalleled, and is a fantastic contribution for intercultural and inter-generational understanding.

Graham Sayer
New Zealand Kendo Federation President
Kendo Kyoshi 7th Dan

Graham Sayer has been president of the New Zealand Kendo Federation since 1987. He attained 4th Dan grade in Japan before moving back to New Zealand in 1985. He has represented New Zealand and competed in Kendo Championships around the world since then. Today he holds the rank of Kyoshi 7th Dan and also serves as auditor for the International Kendo Federation.

Pictorial representation of Musashi's empyreal message in which mastery in all things is achieved by entering the "Ether."

Alexander Bennett, *Bushido Explained*

- THOROUGHLY KNOW THE WAY OF COMBAT STRATEGY
- KNOW VARIOUS ARTS
- A MIND THAT NEVER WAIVERS
- POLISH THE TWO LAYERS OF THE MIND, "HEART OF PERCEPTION" AND "HEART OF INTENT"
- "LOOK IN" (WITH THE HEART) AND "LOOK AT" (WITH THE EYES)

THERE IS GOOD, NOT EVIL IN THE ETHER
THERE IS WISDOM, THERE IS REASON
THERE IS THE WAY, THE MIND, EMPTY

ETHER

A PLACE WHERE THERE IS NOTHING

CLOUDS OF CONFUSION

WHEN THE SPIRIT IS UNCURLED AND COMPARED WITH OVERARCHING UNIVERSAL PRINCIPLES, IT BECOMES EVIDENT THAT A PREJUDICED MIND AND A DISTORTED VIEW OF THINGS HAVE LED TO A DEPARTURE FROM THE PROPER PATH.

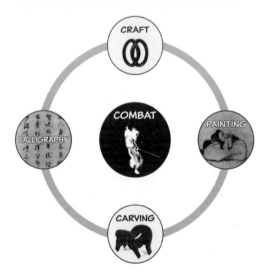

INTRODUCTION

Miyamoto Musashi

The Man, the Myth and the Manuscripts

Miyamoto Musashi (1582–1645) is the most celebrated samurai swordsman of all time. Yet details of his life remain shrouded in mystery.[1] It is precisely this air of mystique, however, that

---

[1] The first mystery is Musashi's real name. From around the thirteenth century onwards, warrior families in the provinces distinguished themselves from other scions of the same clan by adopting the title of their place of residence as their surname. A samurai would have several names during his lifetime depending on age, adoption or changing status, and would often be given a Buddhist name posthumously. In the case of Musashi, his childhood name was Ben'nosuke. For much of his adult life, his formal name was Miyamoto Musashi Genshin (the ideograms for Genshin can also be read as Harunobu). He used "Musashi" on most of his writings and letters until the later years of his life, when he started signing his texts (*Heihō-kakitsuke*, *Heihō Sanjūgo-kajō* and *Gorin-no-sho*) with the surname "Shinmen," inherited from his adoptive father Munisai.

In his first-known text, *Heidōkyō* (1605), he uses "Miyamoto Musashi-no-Kami Fujiwara Yoshitsune." Musashi (the ideograms can also be read as Takezō) was his name but "Kami" indicates an official post (superintendent). (For example, Iizasa Chōisai Ise-no-Kami.) This would then be interpreted as "Fujiwara Yoshitsune Superintendent of the Region of Musashi." He most certainly was not the "Superintendent of Musashi," but adding such a title to one's name was not uncommon. Using the surname of Fujiwara underlined the nobility of his ancestors as the Shinmen could trace their bloodline back to the great aristocratic house. As for "Yoshitsune," it only appears in *Heidōkyō* and was probably a nom de plume inspired by the celebrated warrior Minamoto Yoshitsune (1159–89). More on this shortly. There is also a copy of *Heidōkyō* with a different but similar looking *kanji*

7

adds spice to the fragments of his life story that are known with any certainty.

Like most people, I first became interested in Musashi through reading a popular work of fiction, the 1939 novel

---

ideogram to Yoshi-"tsune" (経) but is read Yoshi-"karu" (軽). This was probably a mistake made in the transcribing process. He was also referred to erroneously as "Miyamoto Masana" in *Honchō Bugei Shōden* (1716). (See the translation by John Rogers.) This may well have been a completely different person. In the same text, "Shinmen" is mistakenly rendered as "Niimi" as an alternative reading. (Also refer to Morita Sakae's *Teisetsu wo Tadasu Miyamoto Musashi Seiden*, reprinted in 2014.)

Much of the confusion can possibly be explained by the theory that there were in fact several swordsmen called "Miyamoto Musashi" who preceded our protagonist. Connected to this theory, the Enmei-ryū school of swordsmanship was not invented by Musashi as is often thought. Legend has it that Minamoto-no-Yoshitsune was taught sublime sills in swordsmanship by the Tengū, a mythological goblin-like creature in Japanese folklore with a long beak and wings, and a man's body, arms, and legs. Yoshitsune in turn taught the skills to the monks of Kyoto's Kuramadera Temple. These monks formed their own independent schools based on Yoshitsune's teachings which became known historically as "Kyō Hachi-ryū," the eight schools of Kyoto. These were often compared to the so-called "Kashima Shichi-ryū," the "seven schools of swordsmanship" that have their roots in the Kashima Shrine in the east of Japan such as Tsukahara Bokuden's Shintō-ryū.

One of the Kuramadera monks called Junjōbō Chōgen created Enmei-ryū. The Okamoto family became custodians of the style of swordsmanship and taught it to warriors in the Shinmen and Hirao clans. A notable early student of the tradition was called "Miyamoto Musashi." Subsequent swordsmen allegedly adopted the name (e.g. Miyamoto Musashi Masana, Miyamoto Musashi-no-Kami Yoshimoto, and Miyamoto Musashi-no-Kami Masakatsu) and it is hypothesized that the moniker became a kind of brand. Munisai's Tōri-ryū may have been based on Enmei-ryū (being related to the Shinmen clan), in which case Musashi's early tuition in swordsmanship would have been an extension of Enmei-ryū. If this was the case, it stands to reason that he would have adopted the name of Miyamoto Musashi when he formed his own version of Enmei-ryū in 1604, as well as the name of "Yoshitsune." For an interesting discourse on the idea of multiple Miyamoto Musashis, refer to Gomi Yasusuke's *Futari no Musashi* (1957).

Genshin (玄信) ideograms have a familial connection with his birth family of Tahara, and were possibly used by Musashi as being symbolic of that link. Musashi's Buddhist name was Niten Dōraku.

Miyamoto Musashi by Yoshikawa Eiji.[2] In this novel, Musashi participates in the pivotal Battle of Sekigahara (1600)[3] as a young teenager alongside his childhood friend, Matahachi. Both naïvely hope to demonstrate their manhood through gallant deeds on the battlefield. They fight for the Western army against the great Tokugawa Ieyasu but their side suffers a disastrous defeat.

Deflated by his experience at the battle, Musashi abandons the material world and throws himself body and soul into the austere life of a dueling samurai swordsman. He is guided in this journey by the famous Zen priest Takuan Sōhō (1573–1645), who appears at critical moments to offer wise counsel, much like Gandalf in *The Lord of the Rings*.[4] Every now and then, a beautiful girl named Otsū appears on the scene and tempts Musashi to give up his martial pursuits for marital ones. In heroic fashion, he resists her charms.[5]

Throughout the novel, Musashi teeters on a knife's edge

---

[2] The English translation by Charles S. Perry is titled *Musashi: An Epic Novel of the Samurai Era* (1981).

[3] The decisive battle in the rise of Tokugawa Ewes, which led to Japan's transition from centuries of war to an epoch of extended peace. Sekigahara is a rustic location in what is now Gifu prefecture. Soon after Toyotomi Hideyoshi died in 1598, powerful *daimyō* lords allied under a tentative veil of stability began to assert their dominance. Two armies readied for war, with the so-called Western Army led by Ishida Mitsunari and the Eastern Army by Tokugawa Ieyasu. Thanks to defections and superior planning, Ieyasu prevailed, leading the way for national unification.

[4] No pun intended. Although contemporaries, Musashi never met Takuan.

[5] Musashi never married. *Dōbō Goen* (1720) by Shōji Katsutomi describes courtesan culture in the Yoshiwara pleasure quarters. One vignette mentions a prostitute called Kumoi who befriended a man named Musashi who "fights with two swords." *Bushū Genshin-kō Denrai* also declares that Musashi had a relationship resulting in the birth of a girl who died aged three. Musashi never wrote of such matters, and details of his love life, if he had one, went to the grave with him. Otsū is purely fictional, but is still celebrated in a Kendo tournament for women in Mimasaka every October.

between life and death, testing his mettle against the most famous swordsmen in the land. He duels the illustrious Yoshioka clan in Kyoto and defeats them all single-handedly through a combination of guile, recklessness and skill. The novel's climax, however, is his celebrated duel with the formidable Sasaki Kojirō on the remote island of Ganryūjima.

Kojirō, armed with a massive sword dubbed the "Drying Pole," waits impatiently for Musashi to arrive by boat from the mainland. However, Musashi bides his time. During the voyage, he whittles a boat oar into a crude but brutally effective club-sword and fastens a band (*hachimaki*) around his head to prevent his hair from falling into his eyes. When the two finally meet on the beach, taunts are exchanged and tension builds. Reaching a crescendo, both men suddenly explode into action, but Musashi triumphs with a perfectly timed blow that crushes Kojirō's skull. At the same moment, the tip of Kojirō's Drying Pole slices Musashi's *hachimaki* in half, nicking his forehead as if to highlight the precision and supremacy of Musashi's skills and the precarious nature of his life as a dueler.

Yoshikawa's novel about Musashi's life and exploits became the blueprint for many subsequent versions of the story in popular culture, including countless comic books, films and television shows. Despite being primarily a work of fiction, Yoshikawa's version of the Musashi story is now assumed by most Japanese to represent something close to historical fact. However, Yoshikawa himself conceded that there were few, if any, trustworthy documents about Musashi in existence, and what little there is "will fill no more than 60 or 70 lines of printed text."

Not overly concerned with historical accuracy at the time, I was irresistibly drawn to the romantic version of Musashi's life depicted in the novel. Having studied the martial art of Kendo (Japanese fencing) in Japan for a year as a high school exchange student, Musashi became for me a kind of imaginary template, and I felt compelled to return to Japan to undertake my own martial quest a year later.

As a naïve teenager, my enthusiasm knew no bounds. Before long, I enrolled at the newly established International Budo University, a specialist martial arts college in Chiba prefecture. I spent the better part of a year there practicing Kendo. I also became acquainted with one of the university professors, Uozumi Takashi, the world's foremost expert on Musashi. It is thanks to his prodigious scholarship that much light has been shed on Musashi in recent years. It was through Professor Uozumi that I learned of Musashi's *Gorin-no-sho*, as well as the philosophy behind his work. I also discovered that the words emblazoned on a scroll hanging in my high school dojo where I first studied Kendo are in fact borrowed from Musashi's philosophy. After each training session, we would recite this verse in unison at the top of our lungs:

"One-thousand days of training to forge,
ten-thousand days of training to refine.
But a [Kendo] bout is decided in a split second."

After a long and illustrious career as a swordsman, establishing and refining his martial skills, followed by years of study in the arts, Musashi retired to the Reigandō Cave in 1643 to meditate and record for posterity his conclusions on the martial way (*heihō no michi*) in *Gorin-no-sho*. In May 1645, a week before he died, he passed the manuscript and all his worldly possessions to his closest disciple, Terao Magonojō. Musashi is credited with other works, including *Heidōkyō* ("Mirror on the Way of Combat," 1605), *Heiho-kakitsuke* ("Notes on Combat Strategy," 1638); *Heihō Sanjūgo-kajō* ("Combat Strategy in 35 Articles," 1641); *Gohō-no-Tachimichi*

("The Five-Direction Sword Pathways," 1642); and *Dokkōdō* ("The Path Walked Alone," 1645). But his most famous work by far is *Gorin-no-sho*.

Musashi's book is arguably one of the most influential and widely read Japanese martial art treatises, not only in Japan but also in the West. It is studied by martial artists for whom the manuscripts were originally intended, and by general readers in Japan and around the world who seek insight into the unforgiving world of samurai warriors. His discourse on strategy has become a guide for modern military leaders as well as corporate warriors attempting to make a killing in the stock market or find success in the competitive world of business.[6] His teachings have even been adopted by experts in the field of sports psychology as a recipe for success in the modern sporting arena.

In *Gorin-no-sho* and other works, Musashi gives few details about his life. He mentions only that his first life-or-death duel occurred at the age of thirteen and that he spent the next fifteen years traveling and dueling throughout the land. Realizing at the end of this period that his triumphs in over sixty mortal contests were due more to luck than to any real knowledge or skill, he reached an impasse.

At the age of thirty, he decided to dedicate the remainder of his life to the pursuit of a greater truth. Following years of austere training and meditation, he eventually saw that the principles for success in swordsmanship and dueling also lead to accomplishment in all other aspects of life. It was this epiphany and wisdom that forms the core message of Musashi's book and what makes it universal, enduring and timeless.

---

[6] For example, see G. Cameron Hurst III's interesting article, "Samurai on Wall Street: Miyamoto Musashi and the Search for Success," Hanover, NH: Universities Field Staff International, UFSI reports no. 44, 1982

The Musashi Myth Industry

An entire industry has grown up around Musashi. This remains very much alive in Japan today, indeed around the world. Musashi is big business and countless people have profited and continue to benefit from his name and reputation. This includes the owners of purported family heirlooms linked to Musashi, who staunchly protect the "authenticity" of their treasures. Others have benefitted from contrived family links that bring prestige upon an entire group or region in Japan. Proprietors of such Musashi relics and places are understandably inclined to ignore any historical facts that may affect their status and accompanying benefits through association.

The otherwise little-known country town of Mimasaka in Okayama prefecture, for example, flaunts the name of their most famous son to attract a steady stream of tourists to "Musashi's birthplace." Curious Musashi aficionados and martial arts groups, foreigners and Japanese alike, keep the local economy afloat as they file through the quaint unmanned "Miyamoto Musashi" railway station, which received its name as recently as 1994.

Recent research corroborated by Professor Uozumi suggests that Musashi was not born in Mimasaka, but this mostly falls on deaf ears in the town. The same can be said, for example, of the proud guardians of "priceless" ink paintings erroneously attributed to the hand of Musashi,[7] who would not welcome an item once valued in the billions of yen suddenly becoming worthless.

---

[7] Authentic Musashi ink paintings are cherished works of art, and several have been designated as National Treasures. Musashi's skill and sensitivity with the brush is undeniable. It is easier to identify fakes these days. Chemically analyzing the paper and ink can determine the work's age. Connoisseurs of Musashi's art can also detect forgeries through the style of brush stroke.

Early Accounts of Musashi's Life

Much of what we know, or think we know, of Musashi's career derives from accounts written long after his death. It is thanks to analysis by scholars such as Uozumi Takashi published in his extensive body of work including *Miyamoto Musashi: Nihonjin no michi* (2002), *Miyamoto Musashi: "Heihō no Michi" wo Ikiru* (2008), and *Teihon: Gorin-no-sho* (2005) that we can draw a more accurate portrayal of who Musashi really was.

To give an example of the Musashi legend, a Kabuki play, "Revenge on Ganryūjima," which debuted in 1737, depicted the duel between Musashi and Kojirō. The play had dramatic though largely fabricated overtones of retribution and was an immediate and long-running hit among townsmen in the main urban centers in early-modern Japan. A later play along similar lines, "Ganryūjima Shōbu Miyamoto" by Tsuruya Nanboku (1755–1829), kept Miyamoto Musashi's daredevil image at the forefront of the popular imagination, as did sundry works of literature, storytelling, puppetry and other art forms.[8]

I am reminded of a famous contemporary film writer named Koyama Kumdo, who decided to write a Kabuki play about Musashi. Koyama hails from Kumamoto where Musashi spent his final days. The plot he devised involved Musashi's time during the Shimabara Rebellion (1637), of which little is known of his exploits. Koyama proposed that Musashi was in fact taken prisoner by the Christian leader of the rebellion, Amakusa Shirō, and that he converted to Christianity. Historically speaking this is a preposterous notion, but such is the nature of Musashi: to this day he inspires people's imaginations

---

[8] There are over forty portraits of Musashi, but even so-called self-portraits were painted around the mid-Edo period so we do not know what he really looked like. According to a passage in *Bushū Genshin-kō Denrai*, Musashi stood six feet tall and was as strong as an ox. If true, he would have been a giant in his day.

in so many ways.[9]

There is no doubt that Musashi was a genius as both a warrior and an artist, but the idealization of his life and achievements is both unnecessary and unintentional in that none of it was his own doing. But, given the basic human desire for drama and heroism, the Musashi legend took on a life of its own, with Musashi transformed into a quintessential swashbuckling superhero of divine proportions. Much of the folklore surrounding him has long been accepted at face value, and the story of his life is now a mishmash of fiction seasoned with a few sprinklings of fact.

Apart from entertainment produced for the masses, pseudo-scholarly renditions of Musashi's life have also contributed to the glorification of the Musashi legend. *Honchō Bugei Shōden* by swordsman Hinatsu Shigetaka, for example, is a widely trusted source of information today regarding great swordsmen of the Edo era and their schools of swordsmanship.[10] Published in 1716, some seventy years after Musashi's death, it was instrumental in forming popular perceptions of Musashi's exploits, in particular his famous duels with the Yoshioka family in Kyoto and with Kojirō on Ganryūjima Island.

In spite of getting Musashi's name wrong (see note 1), Shigetaka's work is more reliable than most as it includes the full text of an inscription found on the famous Kokura Monument,[11] erected in Musashi's honor by his adopted son

---

[9] I was personally asked for my opinion of this thesis by Koyama and immediately presented him with a copy of Professor Uozumi's book *Miyamoto Musashi: Nihonjin no Michi*. As far as I know, the play was never brought to completion.

[10] An English translation of this important work was completed by the late John Rogers. "Arts and War in Times of Peace," 1991.

[11] Kokura is close to Ganryūjima, and the large stone monument was erected there nine years after Musashi's death in 1654 by his adopted son Iori. Given its importance as a primary source, I have included a full translation of the

(and nephew), Miyamoto Iori, nine years after his father's death (see Appendix). However, the dedication offers only a brief synopsis of Musashi's famous duels with the Yoshioka clan and Kojirō. Subsequent materials written decades, if not centuries, after Musashi's death became progressively more detailed, yet provided no corroboration of facts. These narratives need to be viewed with caution.

That said, they are still fascinating to read, and William de Lange did a wonderful job translating the *Bukōden, Bushū Denraiki* and other works in three volumes (*Origins of a Legend: The Real Musashi*, Floating World Editions, 2011).

Of all the works about Musashi, the following two have been the most influential, although much of what is recorded in both is disputable. The first is a substantial biography of Musashi called *Bushū Denraiki* (also *Bushū Genshin-kō Denrai* and *Tanji Hōkin Hikki*), published in 1727 by Tanji Hōkin (also known as Tachibana Minehira).

This book is based on interviews with the third and fourth heads of Musashi's Niten Ichi-ryū school of swordsmanship, and is largely responsible for the popularity of the school and his teachings in the period following his death. The author was the fourth son of Tachibana Shigetani, a vassal of Kuroda Yoshitaka Jōsui, who fought for Tokugawa Ieyasu against anti-Tokugawa forces in Kyushu. Recently discovered primary documents suggest that Musashi himself also served under Kuroda Jōsui in Kyushu rather than at the Battle of Sekigahara, and thus fought for rather than against Tokugawa Ieyasu.

The second account, and the most acclaimed on Musashi's life, is *Nitenki*, published in 1776 by Toyota Kagehide, a senior retainer of the Kumamoto region where Musashi spent his final years. Kagehide's grandfather, Toyota Masakata, was an

---

monument's inscription in the Appendix.

attendant to Nagaoka Naoyuki, who studied under Musashi as a young boy. Masakata collected all the documents he could pertaining to Musashi and passed them on to his son, Toyota Masanaga, who compiled them into the *Bukōden*. Kagehide wrote *Nitenki* based on this compendium.

Each of these chronicles perpetuated the Musashi myth and close inspection shows that their authors took considerable license in filling gaps in Musashi's story. For example, in his *Bushū Genshin-kō Denrai*, Hōkin writes about Musashi's younger years and of a quarrel he had with his father Munisai. Hōkin declares that Musashi showed little respect for Munisai's martial ability. Taking offense at his adopted son's insolence, Munisai threw a short sword at him, and evicted the nine-year-old Musashi from the family home because he turned his "face away and sought to evade danger."[12]

Musashi, according to this account, subsequently went to live with an uncle on his mother's side who was a Buddhist priest. Hōkin also writes of Musashi's alleged aversion to bathing and how he went his entire life without soaking himself after a hard day fighting. Apparently, Musashi claimed that one pail of hot water was enough to cleanse himself. Another explanation is that Musashi felt that being naked in the bath made him vulnerable to attack. Or maybe it was his bad condition of eczema… Such anecdotes have become an established part of the Musashi myth, yet they are not supported by any clear evidence.

Above all, Musashi's duels are described with unbridled fancifulness. As Musashi himself states in *Gorin-no-sho*, his first taste of mortal combat was when he was thirteen against Arima Kihei. It is not known who Arima Kihei was other than that he was a disciple of the Shintō-ryū, a school created by the

---

[12] William de Lange, *The Real Musashi: Bushu Denraiki*, 356/1665 (Kindle).

legendary swordsman Tsukahara Bokuden.

Arima Kihei, Hōkin informs us, was engaged in a warrior pilgrimage (*musha-shugyō*) and made his way to Harima where he posted a sign challenging any local warrior to a duel. This practice was common during an era when itinerant warriors took their killing skills on the road hoping to get noticed and secure a well-paying permanent post in the service of some warlord (*daimyō*). Advertising one's presence with a degree of bellicosity was an accepted part of the game of life and death played by warriors in feudal Japan.

Musashi answered the call and challenged Arima Kihei to a duel. The priest with whom Musashi was now supposedly living was aghast that Musashi, a mere lad of thirteen, could be so audacious. The priest hurried to Kihei's lodgings and begged him to decline, promising that Musashi would be made to apologize publicly. Musashi, however, had different ideas and turned up with a weapon measuring six feet (1.8 meters) in length. Before anybody could stop him, he charged at Kihei, brandishing his weapon like a madman. Kihei drew his blade to deflect the attack but Musashi penetrated his defenses, discarded his staff and unceremoniously dumped Kihei on his head. Barely conscious, Kihei attempted to get back on his feet but Musashi retrieved his staff and beat him to death with fourteen or fifteen blows to the head. Of course, this account was a figment of Hōkin's imagination but nevertheless made for a ripping yarn.

Like Tanji Hōkin, Kagehide was not averse to embellishment and was guilty of piecing together anecdotes from other stories to create an exciting account of Musashi's life. Much of the now standard but erroneous detail of what happened in Musashi's duel with Sasaki Kojirō on Ganryūjima stems from Kagehide's *Nitenki*. For example, the idea that Musashi delayed his arrival on the island to frustrate Kojirō and unsettle his mind is not true. Equally misleading is the commonly held belief that Musashi fashioned a giant wooden sword from an oar as he crossed the strait. Even the surname of his opponent, Sasaki, was not factual but was adopted from a depiction of Kojirō's character in Edo-period plays.

The Modern Musashi Boom

Musashi stories were immensely fashionable throughout the Edo period. It was not until 1909 that Musashi's book, *Gorin-no-sho*, was published for the first time by the Miyamoto Musashi Iseki Kenshō-kai (Miyamoto Musashi Historical Materials Preservation Society, hereafter the Musashi Society). Along with *Gorin-no-sho*, the Musashi Society included other Edo-era documents relating to Musashi, such as *Bushū Genshin-kō-Denrai* and *Nitenki*, to produce what was the first modern encyclopedia of Musashi's life and work, *Miyamoto Musashi*.

Early twentieth-century Japan was politically ripe for some Musashi-style swagger. During the Meiji period (1868–1912), the country had opened its doors to the world. It had also instituted a national educational system which promoted the idea that modern Japanese citizens were the heirs of samurai tradition. This was despite the fact that the class distinctions of the Edo period had been abolished and many descendants of the samurai, who only ever made up 5 to 6 percent of the population, had been washed out to sea in the turbulent current of modernization. Newly created notions of "Bushido" (the Way of the warrior) and of a proud warrior past were propagated vigorously from the 1890s onwards.

The heroic samurai image of yesteryear served the purpose of the new central government that was fanning the flames of nationalism and imperialism in an effort to catch up with advanced Western nations. As anthropologist Harumi Befu points out, "Japan's modernization coincided with the Samuraization process—the spread of the ideology of the ruling warrior class."[13] This was accomplished by introducing a modified "warrior ideology" in the Civil Code and the school curricula through which celebrated warrior customs "permeated the common people."[14]

Books such as Inazo Nitobe's *Bushido: The Soul of Japan* (1900) written in English helped propagate the notion internationally that the Japanese spirit and moral backbone were founded in the culture of the samurai. From the late Meiji period until Japan's defeat at the end of World War II, modern conceptions of Bushido and the martial arts were utilized as an effective educational tool for infusing nationalistic doctrines of self-sacrifice and for bolstering ideas of the Japanese as a powerful warrior race. It was the onset of this social and political climate that heralded a modern Musashi boom.

As discussions about Bushido and the Japanese spirit gathered an enthusiastic public audience, Musashi became a kind of poster boy for samurai culture. Takano Sasaburō, a pioneer in the formulation of modern Kendo included *Gorin-no-sho* in the appendix of his classic book *Kendō* (1913), which became a standard instruction manual for Kendo in schools nationwide. It is from this time that the teachings of Miyamoto Musashi exerted considerable weight in mainstream Kendo philosophy. There are even modern Kendo practitioners who elect to compete with two swords, instead of one, in the tradition of Musashi.

As much as Musashi is revered as a supreme warrior by the

---

[13] See Harumi Befu, *Japan: An Anthropological Introduction*, San Francisco: Chandler Publishing, 1971, pp. 50–52.

[14] Ibid.

majority of Japanese, he is also reviled by some as representing the antithesis of the Way of the samurai. A common criticism is his alleged use of cowardly delaying tactics to irritate his opponents and to win by any means possible, however dishonorable. Although Musashi claimed to have won sixty or so mortal duels, there are few sources that can verify who his opponents were. Does this mean that they were itinerant nobodies in the wrong place at the wrong time? Some scholars maintain that Musashi was little more than a homicidal maniac who killed weaklings for the pleasure of it.

To call somebody a "samurai" in Japan today is to bestow the highest praise. The word epitomizes strength, selflessness, bravery, loyalty and honor. National sports teams such as football, for example, are called Samurai Blue. The baseball team is known as Samurai Japan. To what extent Musashi personified these noble ideals is a matter of opinion. But his reputation as a peerless samurai champion was set in stone long before novelist Yoshikawa Eiji's four-year installments of Musashi's story in the *Tokyo Asahi Shimbun* newspaper. Starting in 1935, the articles were later collated and published as a masterpiece novel simply titled *Miyamoto Musashi*.

With much of the source material taken from the Musashi Society's 1909 publication, the book became a blueprint for a new generation of Musashi movies, radio dramatizations, plays and, more recently, television programs, *manga* comics, and games. Another popular novel called *Miyamoto Musashi* which attempts to depict him in a more "human" light is that by the famous historical novelist Shiba Ryotaro (1968).

The year-long NHK drama about Musashi's life starring seventh-generation Kabuki actor Ichikawa Shinnosuke as the protagonist was popular viewing in Japan in 2003.[15] It sparked

---

[15] Kitano Takeshi played the role of Munisai.

an explosion in domestic tourism to famous historical sites where Musashi's story unfolded, including Mimasaka and Ganryūjima. Also noteworthy is the *manga* artist Inoue Takehiko's highly acclaimed "Vagabond" series. Starting as a serialization from 1998 in the *Weekly Morning* magazine, it was published in 37 volumes in 2014. An English version was published in 2015 and millions of copies have been sold worldwide.

Much of our current knowledge of Musashi is based on educated guesswork. The original manuscript of *Gorin-no-sho*, for example, has never been found. We are forced, therefore, to depend on subsequent handwritten copies, and copies of copies, which contain numerous inconsistencies. There is even disagreement among scholars as to whether *Gorin-no-sho* was authored by Musashi. Some claim it was written by a student after Musashi's death, and he merely signed the manuscript with the master's name. However, the evidence unequivocally shows that Musashi did write *Gorin-no-sho*.

This is where Uozumi's research has been an invaluable contribution to understanding who and what Musashi was. Although the original no longer exists, there are several versions of *Gorin-no-sho* that have survived down the centuries. Uozumi analyzed them with forensic precision to ascertain the historical veracity of each copy and was able to piece together an accurate version of Musashi's original which he published as *Teihon: Gorin-no-sho* in 2005. (My translation is based on this version of the classical Japanese.)

Uozumi discovered two more documents that he believes were also written by Musashi. These are known as *Heidōkyō* and *Heihō-kakitsuke*. The former was already well known, but scholars were uncertain as to whether or not the text could actually be attributed to Musashi's hand. Again, with careful comparison of six existing copies of the text and other related works, Uozumi verified that *Heidōkyō* was indeed written by

Musashi when he was 24 years of age.

Professor Uozumi also uncovered a nameless document he called *Heihō-kakitsuke*, an expose of Musashi's style of swordsmanship when he was in his fifties. He was able to clarify that this too was a work by Musashi, and it went a long way in filling in gaps in our knowledge of how Musashi's swordsmanship evolved, culminating in his *magnum opus, Gorin-no-sho*. All of these texts have been collated and republished in Uozumi's numerous books on Musashi.

Nevertheless, many commentators on the subject of Musashi, and there are many, base their conclusions principally on accounts of his deeds that are historically unreliable. The truth is, nobody knows all the facts. Fortunately, research into sources in recent years by scholars like Uozumi shine more light on Musashi's remarkable life. As new documents are hopefully discovered in the coming years, the truth may become more apparent. In the meantime, I will address what conclusions we can confidently draw about his career, and at the same time put to rest a few misconceptions.

Birth of the Legend: Musashi's Childhood

The following brief outline of Musashi's life draws largely from the meticulous research of Professor Uozumi Takashi, in particular *Miyamoto Musashi: Nihonjin no Michi* (pp. 9–40) and *Miyamoto Musashi: Heihō no Michi wo Ikiru* (pp. 14–22). I have also been a longtime fan of Watatani Kiyoshi's works including the largely forgotten but excellent book *Musashi Matabee: Kyōdo no Kengō-tachi*.

The birthplace, birthdate and parentage of Musashi have long been matters of contention. There are several popular theories. Some people are convinced that Musashi was born in Mimasaka. Others say it was Harima. The regions are in close proximity and Musashi resided in both during his for-mative years. The Mimasaka theory gained momentum in 1909 with the publication of the Musashi Society's book, *Miyamoto Musashi*. It declares that Musashi was the son of Hirata Muni(sai)[16] from the village of Miyamoto, a conclusion based on information contained in recycled material written long after Musashi died and their veracity is questionable.

In Hirata family records reproduced in *Tōsakushi*, Hirata Shōgan is listed as Munisai's father. However, the date given for Shōgan's death falls twenty-six years before Munisai was born. Furthermore, Munisai apparently died two years before Musashi was born. This would make Musashi's birth a miracle of divine proportions! The ideograms used to write "Musashi" in the text are also wrong. They were copied from a Kabuki play popular at the end of the eighteenth century.

A very revealing wooden plaque (*kifuda*) was uncovered in the early 1960s at the Tomari Shrine in Kakogawa City, Hyogo prefecture. The plaque was attached to the inner beam of the shrine to commemorate the completion of restoration work sponsored by the local Tahara family.[17] Hidden from view for three centuries, the 1653 plaque is adorned with an inscription by Iori, Musashi's nephew and adopted son, and it goes some way to solving the mystery of Musashi's family history.

"My ancestors are from the house of Akamatsu, descendants from Tomohira Shinno, the second son of the sixty-second emperor Murakami. At the time of our distant ancestor Akamatsu Mochisada, an official at the Ministry of Justice, the clan fell on hard times. Being forced to shun the name of Akamatsu, they took on the name of Tawara and settled in the village of Yoneda, in the Kanan manor, in the district of Inami,

---

[16] Also known as Muninojō.

[17] Also read as Tabaru or Tawara depending on the region in Japan.

Main Locations in the Life of Miyamoto Musashi

in the province of Harima, where their children and their children's children were born."[18]

Musashi's adoption is also recorded in *Miyamoto Kakei-zu* ("Miyamoto Family Genealogy"), but this document has long been disregarded by scholars because of conflicting dates for the deaths of Musashi's mother and father (1573 and 1577) respectively, which is another physical impossibility since it is also noted that Musashi was born in 1582!

The available documents all have their merits and demerits, some being reconstructed later from memory after the originals were destroyed. Through comparing various source materials, such as the extant Tahara and Miyamoto family records, the Kokura Monument inscription and the Tomari Shrine plaque, not to mention his own admission in the open-

---

[18] See William de Lange's translation in *Miyamoto Musashi: A Miscellany* 158/1916 (Kindle) for a full translation.

ing passage of *Gorin-no-sho* it is almost certain that Musashi was born in Harima, not Mimasaka. Indeed, the most recent and dependable research by Professor Uozumi concludes that Musashi was born the second son of Tahara Iesada of Harima-no-Kuni in a village called Yonedamura.

To add to the confusion, Musashi also mentions in the introduction to *Gorin-no-sho* that, as of the "Tenth day of the tenth month Kan'ei 20 (1643)" he is "sixty years of age." Doing the math, one would assume that Musashi was born in 1584. According to Professor Uozumi, if we interpret "sixty" as an approximation, for example, in his sixties, as was most likely the case, the above-mentioned family records and other documents concur that his year of birth was in fact 1582.[19]

As recorded in the Tomari Shrine wooden plaque, the Tahara family was a branch of the Akamatsu clan, a prominent military family of the Muromachi period (1336–1573). In 1336, Akamatsu Norimura (1277–1350) aligned himself with Ashikaga Takauji, founder of the Muromachi shogunate, and was rewarded for his loyalty with the title of Military Governor (*shugo*) of Harima province and all the privileges that went with the title.

Characteristic of the treachery commonplace in medieval Japan, after learning of the intention of the fourth shogun, Ashikaga Yoshimochi, to gift his land in Harima to his second cousin, Akamatsu Mochisada (?–1427), an enraged Akamatsu Mitsusuke (1381–1441) framed Mochisada. It appears that Mochisada was a "favorite" attendant of Yoshimochi but was forced to commit ritual suicide (*seppuku*) when a rumor was

---

[19] The age of sixty is significant in Japan. The traditional calendar was structured on sixty-year cycles and a new cycle begins on one's sixtieth birthday. As Uozumi postulates, Musashi likely signed off stating his age as sixty as it is considered auspicious and symbolic of the completion of his school of strategy after a lifetime of study. One's sixtieth birthday is celebrated by wearing the color of red in Japan today and is called *kanreki*.

spread, probably by Mitsusuke, that he was having an affair with one of the shogun's concubines.

According to Iori's inscription, the original patriarch of the Tahara family was the very same Akamatsu Mochisada. Akamatsu family records reveal that Mochisada's line ends with his son Iesada, who probably fled to Yonedamura after his father was shamed by Akamatsu Mitsusuke. There is a gap in the family genealogy but it starts again two generations later with Tahara Sadamitsu. Sadamitsu's son was Iesada (not to be confused with his great-great grandfather), the biological father of Genshin (Musashi).[20]

As was the case in the West, embellishing family records was not uncommon in Japan, and it is often impossible to verify the validity of connections with illustrious ancestors once recorded on paper as family lore. Notwithstanding, the most trustworthy sources available at present support the hypothesis that Musashi was born a Tahara, and became the "adopted son" of Shinmen Muninosuke (Miyamoto Munisai) around the age of nine.

An evaluation of the political events of the era suggests that this is a reasonable conclusion. Toward the end of the Warring States period in 1578, Harima became the battleground for Oda Nobunaga's forces led by his right-hand man Toyotomi Hideyoshi. Kodera and other warrior families of the Harima region were defeated by Hideyoshi and the clan was stripped of warrior status.

The Tahara family served the Kodera clan. They were permitted to remain as farmers in defeat but were also forced to relinquish their arms. These measures represented Hideyoshi's early attempts to separate the military from the farming class (*heinō bunri*). His policies eventually resulted in the famous

---

[20] Uozumi, *Miyamoto Musashi: Nihonjin no Michi*, pp. 17–20

"Sword Hunt" (*katana-gari*) later in 1588, and other restrictions to on marriage and free travel. Such a downgrading of status must have been a severe blow for the Tahara and other samurai families of Harima.[21]

Munisai's ancestry can also be traced to the Akamatsu clan. It is likely that Munisai was born into the Hirao family, not Hirata as often stated.[22] A 1689 document covering the history of the Hirao family mentions that following the Kakitsu Incident of 1441 and the consequent fall of the Akamatsu clan,[23] Akamatsu Enshin fled to a place called Hirao in Harima, where he declared himself Hirao Minbu Taiyu and then settled in nearby Ohara. The Hiraos were involved in conflict with the local Shinmen family, who were also of Akamatsu stock. Defeated by the Shinmen in 1499, they were forced to move to another village called Miyamoto. Hirao Tarō'emon was the family head of the fourth-generation Hiraos, and it is he who is thought to have been Munisai.

When Tarō'emon sought employment with the eminent Shinmen clan, he may have thought it wise to drop the Hirao surname considering their somewhat antagonistic past and to

---

[21] Ibid., pp. 22–23

[22] This is a touchy subject I avoid talking about with Hirata Sensei, a good Kendo friend of mine who is very proud of his direct familial connection with Musashi. He is an adamant supporter of the theory that Hirata Munisai was the adoptive father of Musashi. Both the Hirata and Hirao families traced their bloodlines back to the same Akamatsu clan. The Hiratas were vassals of the Shinmen family and they both lived in close proximity in Miyamoto village. Hirata family records were destroyed by fire and later rewritten from memory so it is easy to imagine how confusion could arise.

[23] In 1441, infuriated once again by rumors that the 6th shogun, Ashikaga Yoshinori, also planned to redistribute some of his territories, Akamatsu Mitsusuke took the drastic step of assassinating him at a Noh performance in Kyoto. A shogunal army led by Yamana Sōzen defeated Mitsusuke's forces later that year and Mitsusuke committed suicide after his men deserted him.

replace it with Miyamoto after the place he had settled down.

Tarō'emon proved to be a worthy vassal for the Shinmen clan. He was entrusted with the important task of informing Hideyoshi that the Shinmens pledged allegiance to him. They were subsequently treated favorably for their loyalty following Hideyoshi's triumphant campaign in Harima. Munisai was also rewarded for his feats by being allowed to use the Shinmen name.

Musashi, being the second son of Tahara Iesada, was given up for adoption to Miyamoto (Shinmen) Munisai. In this way, one person at least from the Tahara line would retain samurai status, something that was a matter of pride. It was a logical arrangement considering the tangled strands of the Akamatsu bloodline connecting them all in one way or another.[24]

Thus, Munisai's background is as obscure as Musashi's and most information about him also appears in contradictory texts written long after he died. Many still argue over whether he was a Hirata or a Hirao. Nonetheless, it is evident from what can be pieced together that Munisai was an accomplished martial artist known for his courage in battle. He reputedly took the heads of seven enemy warriors in one battle with a *jūmonji-yari* (crossed pike). As recorded in the *Shinmen-kaki*, "When Muni advanced with his *yari* [lance], seven warriors among the enemy sought to strike Muni down with their *yari*, but he skillfully took hold of their *yari*, running down as many as three warriors, taking their heads and giving chase to the remainder, thereby defeating the Kusakari forces."[25] He created a

---

[24] Throughout his life, Musashi usually referred to himself as Miyamoto. However, in *Gorin-no-sho* he signs off as Shinmen Musashi Genshin, undoubtedly as a reference to his ancestry. On his deathbed he told his student to ensure that the name Shinmen was bequeathed to a future disciple of the Niten Ichi-ryū who demonstrated extraordinary skill.

[25] William de Lange, *Miyamoto Musashi: A Life in Arms*, p. 336/3443 (Kindle).

style of swordsmanship utilizing two swords in unison, which he named Tōri-ryū.[26]

Such was Munisai's renown in battle that he was invited to demonstrate his skill in front of the last Muromachi-era shogun, Ashikaga Yoshiteru. Pitted against the shogun's personal instructor, Yoshioka Kenpō, Munisai won two of the three bouts. This impressed the shogun, who then bestowed on Munisai the lofty designation *Hinoshita Musō* ("Peerless Under the Sun"). It is unknown when Munisai died, but it was most certainly after Musashi's duel with Kojirō for reasons outlined below. Musashi clearly learned his trade under the wing of a formidable warrior.

Forging Mettle

In popular depictions of Musashi's life, he is portrayed as having played a part in the decisive Battle of Sekigahara on October 21, 1600, which preceded the establishment of the Tokugawa shogunate. A more likely hypothesis is that he was in Kyushu fighting as an ally of Tokugawa Ieyasu under Kuroda Yoshitaka Jōsui at the Battle of Ishigakibaru on September 13, 1600. Musashi was linked to the Kuroda clan through his biological birth family who were formerly in the service of the Kodera clan before Harima fell to Hideyoshi.[27]

---

[26] Musashi is often credited with developing the style of combat using two swords simultaneously. This is incorrect. It appears that Munisai passed on dual sword techniques to Musashi and to several other students. There were some subsequent Nitō schools that developed independently of Musashi's line.

[27] The Shinmen and Kuroda clans went against their kin when they aligned with Hideyoshi during the Harima campaign of 1578. It was a topsy-turvy era when allegiances changed frequently. The Shinmen clan fought for Toyotomi supporters against Ieyasu at Sekigahara. The Kurodas, however, fought with Ieyasu's allies in Kyushu. At this juncture, it is likely that

In the aftermath of Sekigahara, Japan was teeming with unemployed warriors (*rōnin*). There are estimates that up to 500,000 masterless samurai roamed the countryside. Peace was tenuous and warlords sought out skilled instructors in the arts of war. The fifteen years between Sekigahara and the first siege of Osaka Castle in 1615[28] was a golden age for *musha-shugyō*, the samurai warrior's ascetic walkabout, but was also a perilous time to trek the country roads. Some *rōnin* found employment as retainers under new masters, some hung up their swords altogether to become farmers, but many continued roving the provinces looking for opportunities to make a name for themselves, which often meant trouble. It was at this point that Musashi embarked on his "warrior pilgrimage" and made his way to Kyoto.

Two years after arriving in Kyoto, Musashi challenged the very same Yoshioka family that Munisai had bettered years before. In 1604, he defeated the head of the family, Yoshioka Seijūrō. In a second encounter, he successfully overpowered Seijūrō's younger brother, Denshichirō. His third and last duel was against Seijūrō's son, Matashichirō, who was accompanied

---

Musashi and Munisai were inadvertently fighting for opposing forces but in different parts of the country. When the Western army was defeated, the Shinmen clan was admitted into the network of Kuroda vassals through their ancestral and regional ties. See Uozumi, *Miyamoto Musashi: Nihonjin no Michi*, pp. 31–32

[28] Tokugawa Ieyasu established the shogunate in 1603. This signified the unification of Japan after centuries of civil war, but the feeling in early Tokugawa Japan was still tense. Unified on the surface only, many harbored feelings of distrust against former rivals and enemies. Hideyoshi's son Hideyori still occupied Osaka Castle, and many a disgruntled *daimyō* not happy with the balance of power developing under the Tokugawas directed their loyalties to the house of Toyotomi. Seeing the Toyotomi and their supporters as a threat, Ieyasu accused them of sedition and mobilized his allies to finish Hideyoshi's legacy once and for all with two all-out attacks on Osaka Castle.

by followers of the Yoshioka-ryū school. Again, Musashi was victorious, and this is where his legend really starts to escalate. Such exploits against a celebrated house of martial artists did not go unnoticed. Allies of the Yoshioka clan wrote unflattering accounts of how Musashi used guile and deceit to win with dishonorable ploys. Meanwhile, Musashi declared himself *Tenka Ichi* ("Champion of the Realm") and must have felt he no longer needed to dwell in the shadow of his father.

On the Kokura Monument, Iori wrote that the Yoshioka disciples conspired to ambush Musashi with "several hundred men." When confronted, Musashi dealt with them with ruthless resolve, one man against many. Although this representation is thought to be relatively accurate, the idea of hundreds of men lying in wait was obviously an exaggeration. Several men, however, would not be hard to believe.

Tested and triumphant, Musashi was now confident enough to start his own school. He called it Enmei-ryū. He also wrote, as confirmed by Uozumi, his first treatise, *Heidōkyō* (1605), to record the techniques and rationale behind them. He included a section in *Heidōkyō* on fighting single-handedly against "multiple enemies," so presumably the third duel was a multi-foe affair.

Originally consisting of 28 articles, the philosophy and nine techniques outlined in *Heidōkyo* were very much centered on those Munisai had catalogued in his school, Tōri-ryū. While his father's influence must have been a clear factor in Musashi's outlook and motivations, *Heidōkyō* was indisputably a product of his own combat experiences. This was, in a way, his grand entrance into the world as a progenitor (*ryūso*) of his own school, and when he started to amass his own disciples.

Ryūha (styles or schools) such as Enmei-ryū did not just appear randomly. There were certain criteria needed for the successful formation and continuation of a *ryūha*. First, not just any warrior could suddenly make his own school on a whim. He had to have extensive combat experience and have a reputation for brilliance that exceeded his peers. In order to gather students, a high degree of charisma and technical proficiency was a prerequisite.

Second, the techniques developed by the *ryūso* had to be effective and proven in battle. They also had to be learnable. A rational and sophisticated set of techniques that could be emulated by anybody who entered the master's tutelage, regardless of physique, needed to be developed in order to be diffused effectively.

Third, the *ryūso* needed to formulate a rational and methodological system for imparting his knowledge to disciples. This was not only to enable disciples to master the techniques, but also to ensure the continuation of the teachings long after the founder had passed away. The teaching methodology would usually revolve around man-to-man teaching of techniques by the master to his disciple(s) utilizing predetermined patterns of movements (*kata*), oral teachings (*kuden*), and, later on in the Edo period, written teachings (*densho*) in the form of scrolls. These were often purposefully vague or elusive to ensure "trade-secrets" were not divulged to outsiders. After his encounter with the Yoshioka, Musashi had clearly met all of these criteria.

Thus, so important was the Yoshioka affair to his career, many accounts exist which embellish the action that took place in Kyoto. In *Nitenki*, for example, details are added such as Musashi's ploy to arrive late for the first two duels, and then take everyone by surprise on the third by turning up early. *Nitenki* also alludes to how the Yoshioka men attacked in great numbers with bows and swords, and that Musashi cut a path through them with only one near miss, when an arrow pierced his clothing.

Another fallacy is the idea that Musashi's victory was the cause of the illustrious Yoshioka clan's downfall. Defeat was surely a stain on their name, but the final nail in their coffin came in 1614. As chronicled in *Suruga Koji-roku*, Yoshioka Kenpō (a different man to Munisai's opponent) exchanged blows with a "disrespectful" guard during a Noh performance in the Kyoto palace and was killed in a showdown later on.

Musashi claims to have engaged in over sixty mortal duels, a large number even for his time. The most celebrated, however, was in 1610 (not 1612 as is usually believed) against Ganryū[29] Kojirō on an island called Funajima (later renamed Ganryūjima).[30] The details of this encounter have long been debated, but the explanation on the Kokura Monument states that the two men met at the designated time. Musashi brandished his 4-*shaku* (121-cm) wooden sword against Kojirō's 3-*shaku* (91-cm) blade. Musashi felled Kojirō with one decisive blow. End of story.

Kojirō was a martial art instructor for the Hosokawa clan in Kumamoto. Known as the "Demon of the West," his reputation in combat was well established.[31] According to *Numata-kaki* (1672), Musashi registered his intent to challenge Kojirō with an elder of the Hosokawa clan, Nagaoka Sado-no-Kami Okinaga (1582–1661). Okinaga then received permission for the duel to go ahead from his lord, Hosokawa Tadaoki (1563–1646).

Given that Kojirō occupied such a prestigious position in the Hosokawa domain, it is surprising that he agreed to such a challenge. He stood to lose everything if defeated. Moreover, if he was killed, there was the distinct possibility that his disci-

---

[29] Literally "Large Rock School."

[30] Refer to Uozumi, *Miyamoto Musashi: Nihonjin no Michi*, pp. 69–85.

[31] *Nitenki* asserts that he was originally a student of the mighty Toda Seigen (1520–?), but again the dates do not add up.

ples would run amok and seek revenge. Being *tozama daimyō*, the Hosokawa family would have been wary of attracting unwanted attention should news of hostilities in their domain reach the shogunate.[32] In spite of this, the duel was sanctioned, but under a strict caveat. It was to take place on a small island called Funajima and the only people allowed to be present were officially appointed witnesses.

An important consideration is why Musashi offered the challenge. Was it a vendetta as often described in popular culture? The *Numata-kaki* (1672) explanation of Musashi's postduel movements provides some important clues. After Kojirō was killed, Musashi made his way to Moji and sought protection in Numata Nobumoto's estate. "It was for this reason, in order to avoid trouble, that Musashi fled to Moji, seeking the help of master Nobumoto, who acquiesced and gave Musashi shelter at his castle, so that the latter was spared."[33]

Nobumoto (1572–1624) was a high-ranking vassal of the Hosokawa domain. According to *Numata-kaki*, Nobumoto escorted Musashi under armed guard to his father Munisai, who was in nearby Buzen at the time. As mentioned above, Munisai began serving the Kuroda clan after the Battle of Sekigahara and had become associated with the Hosokawa clan where he taught swordsmanship to the Kumamoto samurai. Included

---

[32] Ieyasu positioned some of his loyal retainers as *daimyō* and classed them as *fudai* (hereditary vassals). *Fudai daimyō* eventually numbered 145 clans. Another class of *daimyō* were the *shinpan* (cadet *daimyō*), who consisted of blood relatives to the Tokugawa rulers. The remainder were called *tozama* (outside *daimyō*). They were lords who had decided to support Ieyasu's Eastern army just before the Battle of Sekigahara, or those whom Ieyasu saw fit to pardon. Numbering around 100 houses at the end of the eighteenth century, *tozama daimyō* were generally not trusted and were constantly under surveillance.

[33] See *Numata-kaki* translation in William de Lange, *The Real Musashi: A Miscellany*, 493/1916 (Kindle).

among his students was Nagaoka Sado-no-Kami Okinaga, as recounted in *Bukōden*.

Could this mean that Munisai was behind the duel?[34] Some guesswork is unavoidable. If Munisai was teaching his dual sword techniques of the Tōri-ryū to Hosokawa men, this would have riled Kojirō's students. It was not altogether unusual for several styles of swordsmanship to be taught in one domain by different teachers. For example, where I went to school on exchange in Chiba, the Sakura domain once offered five different styles of swordsmanship to its warriors. Same domain or not, however, rivalry between students of different styles could become fractious due to the special bond formed between student and teacher. Taking into consideration the standing of both Munisai and Kojirō as domain instructors, it is hard to envisage that they engaged in any open slander, but overly zealous disciples were a different matter. The whole idea of using two swords at once would have been viewed as peculiar, to say the least, and it is possible that Kojirō's disciples took pleasure in mocking the style (as is the case even today in modern Kendo). Now that the famous Miyamoto Musashi happened to be in Kyushu, the opportunity to taunt Kojirō's students back would have been too good to miss.

In such a tense atmosphere, the Hosokawa authorities may have thought it best to defuse the situation by allowing a duel to go ahead, with Musashi standing in for Munisai. After all, Musashi was not a clansman. If Kojirō won, he would reap the prestige and honor that came with victory and confirm his status as the strongest swordsman in the west of Japan. If he lost, it was to a warrior of great renown. Moreover, once Musashi had gone his merry way, the whole incident would be forgotten.

All accounts of the duel reach the same conclusion.

---

[34] Refer to Uozumi, *Miyamoto Musashi: Nihonjin no Michi*, pp. 70–85.

Musashi's victory is unquestioned. As Uozumi asserts, being an authorized match, it would be unthinkable for Musashi to have employed his infamous sneaky methods and delaying tactics. The duel would have been conducted according to protocol at a designated time and place on the island, with clan officials in attendance to witness the outcome.

Nevertheless, the duel has always been subject to conspiracy theories. It is recorded in *Numata-kaki* that many of Musashi's disciples hid themselves on the island, and that it was they who delivered the final blow to the badly wounded Kojirō. When Kojirō's students got word of this dastardly deed, they went in search of Musashi, bent on revenge, hence the need to escort Musashi away under armed guard. This episode may have been concocted as an appeal to higher authorities, namely by Nobumoto, who took judicious steps to mitigate any escalation of violence in the Hosokawa domain. However, the presence of Musashi's students on the island would have been a serious contravention of the rules.

Nitenki and other texts recount Musashi's duels with many distinguished warriors of the day. As exciting as the stories are, their reliability is debatable. For example, the well-known story about Musashi's use of his short sword in a contest with spear master Okuzōin Dōei probably never happened. Likewise, his duel against the sickle-and-chain wielding Shishidō and his disciples is also famous but questionable. Musashi reputedly defeated Shishidō and his intimidating 10-ft (3-meter) sickle-and-chain by throwing his short sword at his chest. These particular stories, although celebrated, should be assumed to be fictional.

A match that Musashi did have against the strapping "six foot tall" Musō Gon'nosuke in 1605 is described in *Kaijō Monogatari* (1666). According to the account, Musashi smacked the staff-wielding Gon'nosuke in the forehead with a half-finished bow he was making. Conceding defeat, the ever-optimistic Gon'nosuke went on to create the Shintō Musō-ryū school of staff fighting, which is still an influential tradition in stick martial arts (Jodo) today.

There is a shortage of reliable sources sketching Musashi's escapades in the five-year period between the Kojirō duel (1610) and the siege of Osaka Castle (1615). This was probably due to the shogunate's crackdown on unauthorized violent confrontation that could lead to bigger disturbances. Dueling had to remain relatively inconspicuous, at least until protective equipment and fencing methodology was developed in the early to mid-eighteenth century. Whatever the case, it was after the duel with Kojirō that Musashi seems to have changed his focus to pursue a deeper philosophical understanding of the art of war.

The Quest for Higher Awareness

This does not mean that Musashi became a pacifist, nor did he stop participating in combat. In 1615, he fought for the Tokugawa side at the siege of Osaka Castle and then later in the Shimabara Rebellion of 1637. It was thought for a long time that Musashi sided with Toyotomi Hideyoshi's heir, Hideyori, and his supporters during the siege. The recent discovery of a roster of men who fought under the Mizuno banner suggests otherwise.[35] The Mizuno clan was an ally of Tokugawa Ieyasu.

Following the siege, the shogunate promulgated laws limiting each domain to one castle, introduced the *sankin-kōtai* (alternate attendance) system[36] and issued the *Buke Shohatto*

---

[35] T. Uozumi, *Miyamoto Musashi: Heiho no Michi wo Ikiru*, pp. 52–53.

[36] This system was, in effect, a form of hostageship. *Daimyō* were obligated to attend the shogunal palace in Edo at fixed periods, and the expense involved in travelling to Edo was debilitating, as were the costs of maintain-

("Laws for the Military Houses")[37] to determine the responsibilities of samurai under the regime. Such measures were
designed to exert some control over the volatile temperament
of samurai whose very sub-culture had been fashioned over
centuries of violent warfare. The Tokugawa regime was successful in that Japan did indeed pass the next 250 years with
comparatively little conflict.

After the siege, Musashi returned to his area of birth and
settled for a while in Himeji. All *daimyō* in the region—
Honda, Ogasawara, Kuwana from Ise, and Matsumoto from
Shinshū—were newcomers, having been relocated there for
strategic purposes by the shogunate.

Musashi, having useful local connections in the region,
accepted the position of "guest" (*kyakubun*)[38] in the Honda
clan in 1617. The Hondas had been relocated to assume the
governorship of Himeji. As a guest, Musashi was tasked with
teaching swordsmanship. When the shogunate requested that
the Hondas assist the neighboring Ogasawara clan in the construction of Akashi Castle, Musashi was called upon to help
design the surrounding castle town, hence his well-known af-
finity with carpenters. (See the Earth Scroll.)

Around this time, Musashi adopted Mikinosuke, the son

---

ing a mansion for full-time staff, including the *daimyō*'s family members,
who remained in Edo after the lord returned to his domain.

[37] Ieyasu formulated *Buke Shohatto* from thirteen articles with the intention
of defining relationships and obligations of samurai and their houses in
order to maintain lawfulness in the realm. Most of the content was rarely
enforced but it did set official standards of behavior expected of the elite
warrior class.

[38] *Kyakubun* was a position of privilege. It can be equated to a "visiting professor" in the modern university context. A "guest" had no responsibilities in
terms of administration but was expected to share his knowledge with the
daimyō and his vassals in whatever art he had made a name for himself. It
was also a position that gave Musashi a lot of spare time to try his hand at
other artistic pursuits such as calligraphy, ink painting and sculpturing.

of Nakagawa Shimanosuke, Spear Magistrate of the Mizuno clan. Mikinosuke was subsequently appointed as an aide to the Himeji *daimyō's* son, but committed suicide in 1626 following the death of his lord.[39] In the same year, Musashi adopted another son, but this time it was a blood relative. Iori was the second son of Tahara Hisamitsu, Musashi's older brother by four years, and he was retained to serve the Akashi *daimyō*, Ogasawara Tadazane. With his newly adopted son gainfully employed, Musashi became a "guest" of Tadazane and moved to Akashi. Iori was clearly a gifted young man, and five years later, at the age of twenty, was promoted to the distinguished position of "elder" of the domain.

As a guest in the Honda house in Himeji and then the Ogasawara house, Musashi cultivated his artistic expression. He started studying Zen, painting, sculpture and even landscape design, and fraternized with distinguished artists and scholars such as Hayashi Razan. He had a free hand to do as he liked, and he liked to be creative. Having just emerged from an era of incessant warfare, proficiency in the more refined arts had become once again a desirable attribute in high society. It was during this period that Musashi realized how the various arts had much in common in terms of the search for perfection. He understood that the arts and occupations were "Ways" in their

---

[39] With no more battles in which a warrior could prove his worth, there was a marked rise in suicide in the early Edo period. Retainers committed *junshi* (ritual suicide) to follow their lord in death. Such an act was lauded as a supreme demonstration of loyalty and gratitude to the lord, and those who chose this end were honored posthumously. Over time, *daimyō* started to view the number of retainers willing to commit *junshi* as a kind of popularity contest, which in turn led to suicides motivated by peer pressure and bullying rather than genuine loyalty. With the number of officials suddenly dwindling each time a *daimyō* died, the "damned if you do, damned if you don't" custom was condemned by the shogunate, which outlawed the practice by decree in 1663.

own right, by no means inferior to the Way of the warrior. This attitude differs from writings by other warriors, which are typically underpinned by hints of exclusivity, even arrogance, toward those not in "Club Samurai."

That said, the ideal of *bunbu ryōdō* (the two ways of brush and sword in accord) had long been a mainstay of samurai culture. Samurai literature from the fourteenth century onwards exhibits a concern for balancing martial aptitude with the refinement in the genteel arts and civility; namely an equilibrium between *bu* (martial) and *bun* (letters or the arts).

For example, Shiba Yoshimasa's *Chikubasho* (1383) admonishes the ruling class to pay attention to matters of propriety, self-cultivation, and attention to detail. "If a man has attained ability in the arts, it is possible to ascertain the depth of his mind, and the demeanor of his clan can be ascertained. In this world, honour and reputation are valued above all else. Thus, a man is able to accrue standing in society by virtue of competence in the arts and so should try to excel in them too, regardless of whether he has ability or not... It goes without saying that a man should be dexterous in military pursuits using the bow and arrow..."

This was easier said than done in times of constant social turmoil and the chaos of war, but is exactly what Musashi turned his attention to as he entered the twilight years of his life. His pursuit for perfection in both military arts and other artistic Ways is perhaps why he is so revered to this day.

Musashi's Twilight Years

In 1632, the Ogasawara clan were directed by the shogunate to relocate from Akashi to Kokura in Kyushu. Iori, being a house elder, went with them. Musashi followed, retaining his guest status. Five years later, in 1637, the last war of the seventeenth century broke out nearby with the eruption of the Shimabara Rebellion. This was a peasant uprising in the largely Christian Shimabara domain of Matsukura Katsuie. It was sparked mainly by hardship brought on by excessive taxation, famine and religious persecution. Disgruntled *rōnin* and peasants alike joined forces under the leadership of Amakusa Shirō (Masuda Shirō Tokisada, 1622?–38). Shirō was a charismatic youth whose father had served Konishi Yukitaka, a Christian *daimyō* who was killed by Tokugawa Ieyasu in 1600. The "rebels" were besieged by the shogunate's coalition army at Hara Castle on the Shimabara Peninsula. The castle fell in April 1638, and an estimated 37,000 men, women and children were slaughtered.

Iori was given command of over 8,000 troops in the campaign and shone in the theater of battle. Musashi also fought under Ogasawara Tadazane's nephew, Nagatsugu, *daimyō* of the Nakatsu domain, and was put in command of nineteen men. At the front, Musashi became reacquainted with senior officials of the Hosokawa clan from Kumamoto. As a result, he ended up going to Kumamoto two years later, and stayed there for five years until his death.

Little is known about Musashi's actions at the front. Popular accounts emphasize the encounter he had with a humble stone, an event that supposedly nearly ended his life. It says in the *Bushu Denraiki* that he fended off many stones with his staff, as rocks were a common but often underestimated weapon of war in Japan. The source of this rumor can be found in a letter preserved in the Arima family archives. Arima Naozumi a former Christian himself, and *daimyō* of the Nobeoka domain, was in a potentially tight spot on account of some of his former vassals siding with the rebels.

Afraid that the shogunate would view this as guilt by association, Musashi was asked to write a letter as a witness to the heroism demonstrated by Naozumi and his son as they stormed the rebel stronghold before anybody else. Naozumi reneged his faith due to the intensifying persecution Christians faced, so brave though he was, he was not inclined to martyrdom for the sake of a foreign religion.[40]

Musashi states that at the siege of Hara castle his shin was twice struck by rocks, and apologized for not delivering the affidavit in person on account of finding it difficult to stand. It has long been assumed that Musashi was seriously injured, but there is no mention of him in the domain's list of battle casualties. Moreover, he traveled to Nagoya and Edo immediately after the uprising, so any injury he may have sustained was obviously not serious.[41]

Musashi ventured to Nagoya (Owari) and Edo in 1638, possibly in search of employment. Warlords were on the lookout for martial art instructors. Musashi's ability was indisputable. His style of combat, however, did not quite fit the orthodox model of swordsmanship, and so he returned to Kyushu as a guest of *daimyō* Hosokawa Tadatoshi in 1640.

Tadatoshi was roughly the same age as Musashi and adept in both the martial and literary arts. He was among a small handful of elite disciples of the Yagyū Shinkage-ryū who had received a copy of the coveted treatise *Heihō Kadensho* from Yagyū Munenori (1571–1646), an instructor to three generations of shoguns. In fact, Tadatoshi was invited to perform demonstration matches in front of the shogun with Yagyū Jūbei.[42]

It is recorded in *Bukōden* that Hosokawa Tadatoshi summoned Musashi from Kokura in order to see him in action against Ujii Yashirō, a student of Yagyū Munenori and Tadatoshi's teacher of Yagyū Shinkage-ryū. Both duelists were

---

[40] Naozumi's wife was the sister of Ogasawara Tadazane's wife.

[41] T. Uozumi, *Miyamoto Musashi: Nihonjin no Michi*, pp. 110–13.

[42] Yagyū Jūbei Mitsuyoshi (1607–50) was the son of Yagyū Munenori.

required to take an oath forbidding them from disparaging the other's school after the bouts. It is impossible to know exactly what happened, but the author of *Bukōden* records that Musashi fought Yashirō in three bouts. Yashirō was unable to break Musashi's defense. Musashi, on the other hand, contented himself by effortlessly deflecting all that Yashirō threw at him. Tadatoshi was so impressed he also asked Musashi for a match. Equally flummoxed by Musashi's style, Tadatoshi then sought his tutelage.

Being a keen patron of the martial arts, he probably realized that he had much to learn from Musashi, but contrary to what is written in *Bukōden*, it is doubtful if Tadatoshi abandoned Yagyū Shinkage-ryū in favor of Musashi's school. The cultural and political cache that came with affiliation to Munenori's school was far too important to throw away. I will come back to this later. Musashi was permitted to teach in the domain, however, and amassed samurai students of all ranks.

Musashi presented Tadatoshi with a scroll, *Heihō Sanjūgo-kajō*, outlining his teachings in thirty-five articles. Tadatoshi died a month later, which was an emotional blow for Musashi as the pair had grown quite close. Tadatoshi's successor urged Musashi to remain in Kumamoto. He spent the last four years of his life there engaged in practice of Zazen (meditation), painting, and joining tea ceremonies and poetry gatherings with the domain's elite. Many of Musashi's famous ink paintings were created during this period of intense personal reflection.

By this time, Japan had become politically stable and war was now a distant memory. Musashi, being among the last generations who had personally experienced conflict, sensed that samurai were losing their sense of identity. He resolved to make a pilgrimage to Reigandō Cave[43] in 1643 and started writing

---

[43] Literally "Spirit Rock Cave." The sacred spot is situated behind the Ungan-

Gorin-no-sho there, hoping to preserve for posterity his Way, and what he believed to be the very essence of warriorship.

A year later he fell ill, and the domain elders encouraged him to return to Kumamoto to be cared for. He continued working on his treatise for five or six months. On the twelfth day of the fifth month of 1645, he passed the not quite finished manuscript to his student Magonojō. He gave away all his worldly possessions, and then wrote *Dokkōdō*, a brief list of twenty-one precepts that summed up his principles shaped over a lifetime of austere training.

He died on the nineteenth day of the fifth month of 1645. It is said that he had taken ill with "dysphagia," which suggests perhaps that he had terminal stomach cancer. Some say he died of lung cancer. In *Bukōden*, it is recorded that Musashi was laid in his coffin dressed in full armor and with all his weapons. It evokes a powerful image of a man who had dedicated his whole life to understanding the mind of combat and strategy.

As testament once again to the conspiracy theories surrounding Musashi's life, I am reminded of a bizarre book titled *Was Musashi Murdered and Other Questions of Japanese History* by Fudo Yamato (Zensho Communications, 1987). In it the author postulates that Musashi's death was actually assassination through poisoning. The author argues that Musashi and many of his contemporaries such as the priest Takuan, Hosokawa Tadaoki (Tadatoshi's father) who was suspected of "Christian sympathies," and even Yagyū Munenori were all viewed with suspicion by the shogunate. He goes so far as to hypothesize that the phrase found at the end of Musashi's

---

zenji Temple in west Kumamoto, which dates back to 1351. In the center of the shallow cave is a large boulder of volcanic rock which is referred to as the "meditation stone." At the back is an enshrined statue of the four-faced goddess Kannon. Legend has it that the statue mysteriously washed up at the cave 1,000 years ago after the ship that was transporting it sank.

Combat Strategy in 35 Articles "Should there be any entries you are unsure of, please allow me to explain in person…" was actually interpreted by the government as a call for those with anti-shogunate sentiments to gather in order to hatch a seditious plot (p. 20). This is why, Fudo Yamato argues, Musashi and these other notable men of his age all died mysteriously at around the same time.

Musashi's Swordsmanship

Musashi established his Enmei-ryū school in 1605. This early school continued even after he renamed his style of swordsmanship Nitō Ichi-ryū, and finally Niten Ichi-ryū. Enmei-ryū had gained a following in the domains of Himeji, Tatsuno, Hiroshima and Owari, where Musashi had spent some time throughout his wanderings. One of Musashi's earliest known students in the Enmei-ryū was Tada Yorisuke, who studied under him from 1615 to 1624. Of the many adherents of Musashi's early school, Aoki Jōeimon was an outstanding swordsman who later created the Tetsujin-ryū in Edo and is said to have had a following of nearly 9,000 students.[44]

In Himeji, where Musashi spent his later thirties as a guest of the Honda clan, Enmei-ryū was adopted by Honda Tadamasa as one of the schools of swordsmanship to be taught to samurai in the domain. In *Bisan Hōkan*, it is recorded how Tadamasa was keen to test Musashi with the intention of making him a retainer if rumors about his superb skills proved to be true. He instructed Miyake Gunbei (or Gundayū) of the Tōgun-ryū, a stalwart in the domain, to challenge Musashi. When Miyake called in at Musashi's lodgings he was let in,

---

[44] With fame came fraud, and many schools sprang up claiming to be directly transmitted from Musashi, but were in fact not.

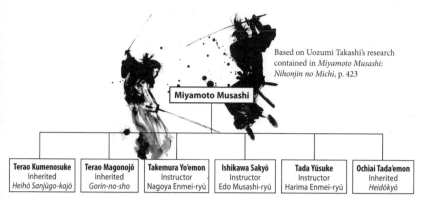

Based on Uozumi Takashi's research contained in *Miyamoto Musashi: Nihonjin no Michi*, p. 423

Miyamoto Musashi

Terao Kumenosuke	Terao Magonojō	Takemura Yo'emon	Ishikawa Sakyō	Tada Yūsuke	Ochiai Tada'emon
Inherited	Inherited	Instructor	Instructor	Instructor	Inherited
Heihō Sanjūgo-kajō	*Gorin-no-sho*	Nagoya Enmei-ryū	Edo Musashi-ryū	Harima Enmei-ryū	*Heidōkyō*

but to his annoyance was kept waiting for an hour or so while Musashi played chess with another guest. When Musashi realized that Gunbei's purpose was to challenge him in a bout, he nonchalantly agreed and asked his would-be opponent to choose between live blades or wooden swords. Gunbei chose the safer option, wooden swords, but received a very bloody mouth for his troubles. Tadamasa subsequently invited Musashi to join his ranks but he declined and became a guest of the Honda domain instead.

Musashi's travels to Nagoya are mentioned in *Mukashi-banashi* (1758?) by tea master Chikamatsu Shigenori of the Owari domain. Musashi was invited by Tokugawa Yoshinao to demonstrate his style against experts of the Yagyū Shinkage-ryū, the predominant school in the region. Musashi fought with two swords and forced his opponent backward with the tip of his long sword directed menacingly at his nose. No swordsman could get the better of him. His dominance over local warriors was enough for Musashi's Nitō Ichi-ryū, as it was called then, to take root and flourish in Owari. A translation of this episode can be found in de Lange's *The Real Musashi: A Miscellany*.

Musashi is also mentioned in *Hayashi Razan Bunshū* (1662),

a collation of memoirs by the great neo-Confucian scholar Hayashi Razan (1583–1657). "The swordsman Shinmen Genshin wields a sword in each hand and calls his school of swordsmanship Nitō Ichi-ryū" (de Lange). This would have been around 1638–39. Musashi refers to his school as Nitō Ichi-ryū in *Heihō Sanjūgo-kajō* (1641). In *Gorin-no-sho* he uses both appellations, Nitō Ichi-ryū and Niten Ichi-ryū, and it seems he was still in the process of rewriting the manuscript to reflect his school's name change in favor of the latter. Thus, it was at the very end of his life in Kumamoto that the school became "School of Two Heavens as One" instead of "Two Swords as One."[45] Compared to his younger, more rambunctious days, the early techniques he developed in the Enmei-ryū and catalogued in *Heidōkyō* had matured into an art of awe-inspiring refinement and effectiveness.

Although the typical image of Musashi implies that he was a savage fighter, Terao Magonojō is quoted in *Bukōden* describing Musashi's swordsmanship as "exceptionally serene, as if one were watching a performance of Noh." Of all Musashi's students, Magonojō was his favorite, at least in his twilight years. Partially deaf and unable to serve as a retainer in the domain, Musashi took a liking to Magonojō, who spent his time at his master's side studying the way of the sword. Magonojō's brother Motomenosuke (Kyūnosuke) was also a talented student and was tasked with looking after Musashi as his health started to fail.

Motomenosuke later became the head instructor for swordsmanship in the Kumamoto domain where he contin-

---

[45] Musashi's school is often translated as "Two Swords/Heavens One School." I think that this rendition is missing the point of using dual swords in unison. Musashi emphasized the importance of things converging, which is why I believe "School of Two Swords/Heavens as One" is closer to Musashi's philosophy.

Transition of Techniques in Musashi's Schools and Writings

Table based on Uozumi Takashi's research in *Miyamoto Musashi: Nihonjin no Michi*, p. 117

Heidōkyō (兵道鏡) 1605	Nagoya Enmei-ryū School (名古屋円明流)	Heihō-kakitsuke (兵法書付) 1638	Gorin-no-Sho (五輪書) 1645	Heihō 39 (兵法三十九箇条) 1666
Technique Names Tachi-no-Mei Omote 太刀の名表	Forms Omote 表	Five Sword Stances Tachi Kamae Itsutsu-no-Koto 太刀構五つの事	Five Exterior Forms Itsutsu-no-Omote 五つのおもて	Five-way Stances Goho-no-Kamae 五方の構
1. Sashiai-giri 指合切	1. Enkyoku 円曲	1. Enkyoku 円曲	1. Daiichi-no-Koto (Chūdan) 第一の事 中段	1. Katsu-totsu Kissaki-gaeshi (Chūdan) 喝咄切先返 中段
2. Tenpen-no-Kurai 転変之位	2. Katsu-totsu 喝咄	2. Gidan (Jōdan) 義断	2. Daini-no-Koto (Jōdan) 第二の事 上段	2. Gidan (Jōdan) ギダン 上段
3. (Same) Uchi-otosaruru-Kurai 同打落さる>位	3. Yo-ken (Yang) 陽剣	3. Shigeki (Gedan) 鷲撃	3. Daisan-no-Koto (Gedan) 第三の事 下段	3. Uchoku (Right-side) ウチョク 右脇
4. In-no-Kurai & Katsu-totsu 陰位 付 喝咄	4. In-ken (Yin) 陰剣	4. Uchoku (Left-side) 迂直	4. Daiyon-no-Koto (Left-side) 第四の事 左脇	4. Shigeki (Left-side) 重気 左脇
5. Yo-no-Kurai & Evasion 陽位 付 貫く心持	5. Suikei 水形	5. Suikei (Right-side) 水形	5. Daigo-no-Koto (Right-side) 第五の事 右脇	5. Suikei (Gedan) スイケイ 下段
6. (Same) Harutsumori 陽位 付 はる積				*All added to Heihō 35 by Terao Kumenosuke in 1666
7. Jokato 定可当				

49

ued the tradition of Niten Ichi-ryū. His son, Nobumori was a prodigy martial artist, considered to be the reincarnation of Musashi. He was thus chosen to adopt Musashi's surname, Shinmen. Magonojō's line of the Niten Ichi-ryū ceased after one generation in Kumamoto, but his student Shikata Sanzaemon transferred to Fukuoka and taught the tradition there. Kumenosuke's line continued in Kumamoto. There are several lines of Niten Ichi-ryū that survive today, and even Enmei-ryu is also practiced by a small group of enthusiasts in Japan.

As with many other martial art schools during the Tokugawa period, scroll forgeries for Muasashi's school were not uncommon. As it is virtually impossible to verify authenticity in many cases, factions claiming legitimacy and hence superiority over other lines have continued through the centuries to this very day. This is a common problem plaguing many different schools of classical martial art schools.

The "Five Ring" Scrolls in Context

Musashi's *Gorin-no-sho* places the study of swordsmanship and strategy at the very center of the warrior's being, as he himself had done throughout his own life. As the name suggests, *Gorin-no-sho* (literally "Five Ring Scrolls") consists of five scrolls. Each scroll takes the name of one of five universal elements: *Chi* (Earth), *Sui* (Water), *Ka* (Fire), *Fū* (Wind) and *Kū* (Ether). Interestingly, it was *Heihō Sanjūgo-kajō (Heihō 35)* that served as the transmission scroll in the Kumamoto Niten Ichi-ryū rather than *Gorin-no-sho*. In other words, *Gorin-no-sho* was not handed down to successive heads of the school as its official teaching license. Magonojō was the recipient of Musashi's original manuscript. His line of the school relocated to Fukuoka with the second generation, and *Gorin-no-sho* was used for transmission of the school there, but nowhere

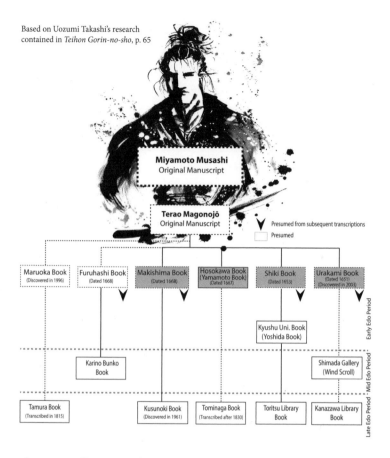

Based on Uozumi Takashi's research contained in *Teihon Gorin-no-sho*, p. 65

else. Few adherents of the Niten Ichi-ryū even knew about the scrolls, let alone had read them.

Sadly, the original manuscript of *Gorin-no-sho* no longer exists. According to Terao Magonojō, it was destroyed in a castle fire, possibly the Edo Castle fire of 1657 or the Yashiro Castle fire in Kyushu in 1672. Musashi never titled the five scrolls *Gorin-no-sho*. He named each individual scroll as one of the five elements. It was Nagaoka Naoyuki and Toyota Masakata who conceived *Gorin-no-sho* as a shorthand title in their notes, and this designation stuck.

As for the use of the "five elements" (*gorin*), it was not Musashi's intention to appropriate the idea from Buddhist philosophy. In *Heihō Sanjūgo-kajō*, he had already referred to the heart or mind of the warrior as being comparable to the properties of "Water." He also wrote briefly of the "Ether" as a state of high attainment and clarity, but not in the Buddhist sense of Nirvana. It was more like figuratively piercing through the clouds of confusion and being exposed to the boundless clear sky.[46] Moreover, he had discussed the "Wind" of other schools in previous texts. Wind is a term in Japanese indicating "type" or "appearance." Adopting "Earth" to explain the basis of his school, and "Fire" to represent what happens in the heat of battle and dueling, probably seemed convenient and oddly prophetic.

To date, only ten handwritten copies (*shahon*) containing all five scrolls have been found. The principal one used in modern publications is the Hosokawa Book, which was transcribed twenty-two years after Musashi's death, possibly from one of Magonojō's copies. Uozumi Takashi found five sections to be absent in the Hosokawa Book and over 150 miscopied characters. He compared all the extant copies to identify discrepancies and commonalities, and extrapolated a standard text which is estimated to be the closest in content to Musashi's original, and why I chose this as the basis for translation.

The Content of Gorin-no-sho

In "Earth," Musashi documents the first half of his life. He also introduces military tactics and the metaphysics behind his school. He asserts that combat strategy is applicable to both generals and rank-and-file soldiers. He also includes a set of

---

[46] The ideogram used for *kū* (空) is also read as *sora* (sky).

rules the warrior should follow if he is serious about mastering the Way.

In "Water," Musashi explains various aspects of individual combat, such as mental and physical posture, gaze, how to manipulate the sword, footwork and fighting stances. The content is pragmatic and provides aspects of sword work in detail.

In "Fire," he expounds on such matters as how to choose the best site for dueling, how to control the enemy by taking the initiative and implementing stratagems not only applicable to one-on-one duels but also to large-scale battles involving thousands of men.

In the fourth scroll, "Wind," he critiques other schools of swordsmanship and summarizes their weaknesses. Finally, "Ether" is a short and somewhat nebulous section. He discloses the supreme level of all arts by referring to the allegorical "void," "emptiness" or "nothingness." He describes the state of emptiness that the warrior must achieve in his own mind in order to find "liberation."

Musashi's illustrious contemporary, Yagyū Munenori, wrote the aforementioned *Heihō Kadensho* ("Book on Family Transmitted Military Arts") in 1632. It is useful to compare this with Musashi's *Gorin-no-sho* to understand the merits of each. *Heihō Kadensho* represents a complex fusion of technical teachings on the swordsmanship of Muneyoshi, Munenori's father, and Kamiizumi Ise-no-Kami, founder of the Shinkage-ryū, and is heavily influenced by Noh and Zen ideals. Teachings of the celebrated Zen priest Takuan Sōhō also feature prominently. An advisor and spiritual teacher to Munenori, many of Takuan's observations were included almost verbatim in *Heihō Kadensho*.

Munenori's well-received exposition takes a complex and deeply psychological approach to combat. It held considerable sway with his powerful disciples who occupied the upper echelon of samurai society. It provided them with a basis for their study of swordsmanship and, more importantly, guidelines for nurturing their political astuteness for governance. It was one of the first important martial texts in Japan that organized the training of body and mind into a systemized holistic corpus for combat, life and governance.

There are similarities between Munenori's and Musashi's work. For example, the emphasis both place on mindset in combat, how mastery of strategy entails a lifelong regime of diligent practice, and how it applies to other facets of life. What makes Musashi's treatise distinctive is the way he draws parallels between the disciplines of combat and other arts and vocations, such as carpentry. His overall thesis is, on the surface, simpler than Munenori's. Musashi does not dwell on obscure Zen or Confucian concepts. Even though the "five elements" point to Buddhist doctrine, this was not Musashi's intention. What he means by "Ether," for example, is "a place where there is nothing" in comparison with "a place where there is something," that is, a clear sky as opposed to a cloudy sky.

As a set, the five scrolls are well organized and accessible. Whereas Munenori, a *daimyō* himself, wrote his treatise for warriors of the highest status, Musashi was really only concerned with the welfare of his students, some of whom were not in the service of a lord. Musashi takes an overtly critical stance toward other schools and points out weaknesses to be exploited and not emulated. Such denunciation of other styles is not present in Munenori's work. Musashi's book is down to earth and clearly formulated through years of dangerous toil. You can almost smell the stench of combat in the text. Munenori's treatise, on the other hand, emits erudition and refinement, fortified by strong allusions to religiosity. (Refer to my book *Kendo: Culture of the Sword* for a detailed analysis.)

Musashi started with techniques that were easy for novices

to learn. Then they would tackle more advanced principles. The combat theories championed in the Water and Fire Scrolls are well defined and designed to purge the student's mind of presumptions and bad habits. This way, the swordsman can be left to his own devices, eventually reaching a level where his spirit is clear and devoid of bias. He called this the "Direct Path," and *Gorin-no-sho* provides the procedures to keep on the right track stressing that without forging the mind and body through years of training, there is no chance of success. With the direction mapped out, it is left to the reader to add blood, sweat and tears to the equation, and find his own Way.

Conclusion

There are several English translations of *Gorin-no-sho* but they are of varying reliability. The first was by the late Victor Harris in 1972. A recent and very readable version, *The Five Rings: Miyamoto Musashi's Art of Strategy*, was published by my colleague David Groff in 2012. What makes my translation different to the others, however, is that it is based on Uozumi Takashi's ground-breaking scholarship in recreating the closest conceivable text to Musashi's original. In addition to Musashi's earlier works, *Heihō Sanjūgo-kajō* (1641) and *Dokkōdō* (1645), I have included other texts attributed to him that have not previously been translated: *Heidōkyō* (1605), *Heihō-kakitsuke* (1638) and *Gohō-no-Tachimichi* (1642). The inclusion of these manuscripts will show how Musashi's principles evolved over the course of his career.

Finally, having studied Kendo and the history of martial culture in Japan for three decades now, I feel that I have reached a stage in my own "austere training" where I can do Musashi's work justice linguistically, spiritually and technically. We modern Kendo exponents do not, of course, wander the world seeking to engage in mortal combat. Nonetheless, Musashi's teachings are very much alive and central to the study of Kendo. Being fifty years old now, the age at which Musashi declared he had finally grasped the meaning of the Way, his wisdom resonates with me now more than I could have ever imagined when I first read *Gorin-no-sho* thirty years ago.

I hope that this translation will be of interest to a broad range of readers, from historians to martial arts enthusiasts and aficionados of Japanese culture. Any and all mistakes in the text are solely my own.

The following table of Musashi's life events is based on Uozumi Takashi's *Miyamoto Musashi: Nihonjin no Michi* (pp. 55–57). Note that as his year of birth as established by Uozumi was 1582 (not 1584), other events need to be adjusted accordingly.

Year	Event
	• **Kamakura Shogunate 1185–1333** • **Muromachi Shogunate (also known as Ashika-ga Shogunate) 1336–1568** **Warring States Period (*Sengoku jidai*) 1467–1568** **Azuchi-Momoyama Period 1568–1600** • **Edo Shogunate (Tokugawa Shogunate) 1603–1868**
1582	Musashi born in Harima's Yonedamura Village as the second son of Tahara Iesada.
1585	Toyotomi Hideyoshi becomes Regent.
1585	Musashi adopted by Miyamoto Munisai of Mimasaka due to common ancestral connection to the Akamatsu clan.

Year	Event
1594	First experience in combat with Arima Kihei of Shintō-ryū.
1597	Defeats Akiyama of Tajima in a duel.
1598	Receives a teaching license in the Tōri-ryū from Munisai.
1600	Battle of Sekigahara. Musashi serves the Tokugawa allied Kuroda clan in Kyushu, not on the side of Ishida Mitsunari as is often assumed.
1602	Starts his "warrior pilgrimage" (*musha-shugyō*) and journeys to the capital, Kyoto.
1603	Tokugawa Ieyasu establishes the shogunate in Edo.
1604	Musashi fights the illustrious Yoshioka family in a series of duels making a name for himself.
1605	Establishes the Enmei-ryū school of swordsmanship and writes *Heidōkyō* as one of the first martial art textbooks. Spends the next five years engaging in over 60 duels.
1610	Defeats Kojirō in a duel on Ganryujima Island (Funajima).
1611	Musashi reflects on his career and laments that he does not truly understand the principles of combat.
1615	Participates in the Summer Siege of Osaka Castle as a warrior of the Tokugawa-affiliated Mizuno clan against the last Totoyomi stalwarts.
1617	Becomes a guest of the Honda clan in Himeji. His adopted son Mikinosuke serves Honda Tadatoki.

Year	Event
1618	Helps design the township around Akashi Castle and engages in various artistic pursuits.
1626	Honda Tadatoki dies of illness and Mikinosuke commits ritual suicide to follow his lord in death (*junshi*). Musashi's second adopted son, Iori, enters the service of the Ogasawara clan in Akashi and Musashi becomes a clan guest.
1631	Iori becomes an elder (*karō*) of the Ogasawara clan.
1632	The Ogasawara clan relocates from Akashi to Kokura in Kyushu. Musashi and Iori accompany them. Yagyū Munenori writes *Heihō Kadensho*.
1638	Musashi participates in the Shimabara Rebellion with Iori where he sustained an injury by being hit by a rock. Writes *Heihō-kakitsuke*. Travels to Nagoya and Edo.
1640	Guest of the Hosokawa clan in Kumamoto.
1641	Presents *Heihō Sanjūgo-kajō* to Lord Hosokawa Tadatoshi who dies one month later.
1642	Writes *Gohō-no-Tachimichi*.
1643	Begins writing *Gorin-no-sho*.
1645	Passes the *Gorin-no-sho* manuscript to his student Terao Magonojō. Writes *Dokkōdō*. Dies on the 19th day of the 5th month.

THE BOOK OF
FIVE RINGS

GORIN-NO-SHO

五輪書

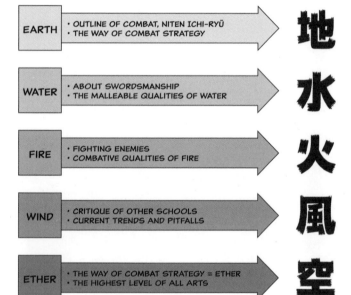

EARTH	• OUTLINE OF COMBAT, NITEN ICHI-RYŪ • THE WAY OF COMBAT STRATEGY
WATER	• ABOUT SWORDSMANSHIP • THE MALLEABLE QUALITIES OF WATER
FIRE	• FIGHTING ENEMIES • COMBATIVE QUALITIES OF FIRE
WIND	• CRITIQUE OF OTHER SCHOOLS • CURRENT TRENDS AND PITFALLS
ETHER	• THE WAY OF COMBAT STRATEGY = ETHER • THE HIGHEST LEVEL OF ALL ARTS

地
水
火
風
空

The Earth Scroll
Chi-no-Maki
地 の 巻

Main Points

* *The Way of Combat Strategy broadly denotes the samurai's way of life and social obligations.*

* *Musashi makes no distinction between samurai and the other classes in terms of preparedness to sacrifice life for the sake of honor.*

* *Each occupation is a "Way" in its own right. What sets the samurai apart from other echelons of society is that their Way demands victory at all costs.*

* *Musashi compares the samurai general with the master carpenter in his theory of leadership.*

* *The meaning behind Musashi's school of swordsmanship, the Niten Ichi-ryū, is explained.*

* *Nine rules for following the Way of Combat Strategy are provided.*

* *Translation source is Uozumi Takashi's* Teihon Gorin-no-sho, *pp. 73-94.*

Introduction

I call my Way of combat strategy[1] Niten Ichi-ryū.[2] This being the beginning of the tenth month of Kan'ei 20 (1643), I have climbed up Mount Iwato in the province of Higo in Kyushu,[3] paid homage to Heaven, made a pilgrimage to Kannon, and face the altar as I contemplate writing down for the first time the culmination of what I have learned over many years of austere training.[4] A warrior of Harima, my name is Shinmen Musashi-no-Kami Fujiwara-no-Genshin. I am sixty years old.[5]

I have devoted myself to studying the discipline of combat strategy since I was young. I experienced my first mor-

---

[1] I have translated *heihō no michi* as the "Way of combat strategy." *Heihō* (also read *hyōhō*) is a prevalent term throughout *Gorin-no-sho* but it can have different meanings. Written with the two ideograms of *hei* (兵) = soldier and *hō* (法) = law or method, in the broader sense it encompasses the necessary skills for a warrior, such as knowledge of strategy and warfare. In the narrow sense, *heihō* denotes swordsmanship (*kenjutsu*). Combined with *michi* (Way), it also means the code by which warriors live, and this was at the heart of what Musashi meant by *heihō no michi*.

[2] Musashi's school was named Niten Ichi-ryū (School of Two Heavens as One), but in the Fire, Wind and Ether scrolls he refers to it mostly as Nitō Ichi-ryū (School of Two Swords as One). He rewrote the draft of the Earth Scroll but not the others before passing the manuscripts to his disciple, Terao Magonojō a week before his death. This suggests he was about to change all references from "Nitō" to "Niten." It should be noted that following the tradition of Miyamoto Musashi, there are a small number of practitioners in modern martial arts (Kendo) who compete with both a short and long bamboo sword (*shinai*) in what is called Nitō. The classical school(s) of Musashi's swordsmanship that are continued today, however, refer to themselves as Niten Ichi-ryū.

[3] Kumamoto.

[4] Kannon (Kwannon), meaning "the one who hears their cries," is known in Sanskrit as Avalokiteçvara. In Japan, Kannon was one of the most popular of all bodhisattvas. Personifying "compassion," Kannon was believed to deliver all beings from danger when her name was invoked.

[5] The original Japanese states "sixty" but should be interpreted as sixty something. This previously caused confusion about his year of birth. (See Uozumi, *Teihon Gorin-no-sho*, p. 174 for more details.)

tal contest at thirteen[6] when I struck down an adherent of the Shintō-ryū[7] named Arima Kihei. At sixteen, I defeated a strong warrior named Akiyama from the province of Tajima. At twenty-one, I ventured to the capital [Kyoto] where I encountered many of the best swordsmen in the realm.[8] Facing off in numerous life-and-death matches, I never once failed to seize victory. Afterward, I trekked through the provinces to challenge swordsmen of various systems and remained undefeated in over sixty contests. This all took place between the ages of thirteen and twenty-eight or -nine.[9]

After turning thirty, I reminisced on past experiences and realized that my success could not be credited to a true mastery of strategy. Could my triumphs have been attributed to an innate ability in the Way of combat strategy that kept me from straying from Heavenly principles? Or was it due to flaws in the other schools of swordsmanship that I encountered? Thereafter I studied zealously from morning to night

---

[6] Musashi started studying the martial arts in earnest under his adoptive father, Miyamoto Munisai. Munisai established his own school called Tōri-ryū, which specialized in the small-bladed truncheon (*jitte*), and it was in these techniques that Musashi got this start in the art of combat. See my translation of the Kokura Monument in the Appendix on page 151. Documents point to Munisai as being the first to pioneer fighting with two swords.

[7] Established by the celebrated warrior Tsukahara Bokuden, the Shintō-ryū was one of the earliest established martial art schools (*ryūha*) in Japan.

[8] This would have been 1602, one year before the Tokugawa shogunate was started by Tokugawa Ieyasu (1603). His three encounters with the renowned Yoshioka family, teachers of the arts of war to the Muromachi shoguns, are widely known and contributed greatly to his rising fame. Following his triumphs against the Yoshiokas, he announced the creation of the Enmei-ryū school, and also wrote his first treatise, *Heidōkyō*. See translation in Appendix 1. This passage also refers to other itinerant warriors seeking to make a name for themselves through their dueling prowess.

[9] By his own admission, Musashi's last duel was his legendary encounter with Kojirō on Ganryūjima Island.

in a quest to discover the deepest principles. I was about fifty when I realized the real meaning of the Way of combat strategy. Since then, I have spent my days not needing to seek any more. Having attained the essence of the Way of combat strategy, I practice the disciplines of many arts without the need of a teacher in any of them.

As I write this dissertation, I do not appropriate terms from Buddhist law or Confucian teachings, nor do I quote old customs from ancient war chronicles and military texts in conveying the perceptions and true spirit of my school.[10] With the Heavenly Way and Kannon as my mirror, I put brush to paper and commence writing this evening on the tenth day of the tenth month in the hour of the Tiger.[11]

To begin with, combat is the mandate of warrior houses. It is incumbent on the general to practice the Way and for soldiers who fight under him to know it. No warriors these days perfectly understand what the Way of combat strategy really entails.

First, of the myriad disciplines in the world Buddhist law is the Way of salvation. The Way of Confucianism specifies precepts for those engaged in the Way of letters. Physicians practice the Way of healing various ailments. There are po-

---

[10] Many of the military texts in existence in Musashi's time cited ancient Chinese classics and incorporated arcane Buddhist or other religious concepts to explain the deeper principles of the tradition. Yagyū Munenori's *Heihō Kadensho* is a good example. This gave the schools an air of divinity and legitimacy. Indeed, Musashi's earlier texts, *Heidōkyō* and *Gohō-no-Tachimichi*, contain quotations from well-known ancient Chinese texts. In *Gorin-no-sho*, he clearly states his intention to explain the principles of his school in his own words, in a very matter-of-fact way without using mysterious religious terms. Although he refers to the "Heavenly Way" and Kannon in the very next sentence, this is probably inferring that his combat principles represent the universal laws of nature.

[11] While he states it is "evening," the hour of the Tiger represents the dawn hours between 4:00 and 4:30.

ets[12] who teach the Way of *waka*.[13] Then there are those who practice tea, archery, protocol and other artistic Ways.[14] In all of them, followers study their chosen discipline as they please and do so because they enjoy it. There are few, however, who practice the Way of combat because they like to.

To start with, as the term *bunbu-nidō* suggests,[15] the correct Way for warriors is to possess the desire to practice the arts of both scholarship and war. If, for example, the warrior proves inept, he must make every effort to excel in his Way in accordance with his social standing.

Inquiring into the minds of samurai today, it would seem that many believe the warrior's Way demands nothing more than an unwavering preparedness for death. The Way of death, however, is by no means limited to the domain of the samurai. Priests, women, farmers and those beneath them[16] are also aware of their social obligations and embody a sense of shame. They, too, are prepared to sacrifice life when the time comes, making them no different from samurai.[17]

For those practicing the Way of combat strategy, however, being better than others in everything is fundamental. The warrior must prevail when crossing swords with a single opponent and be victorious in a mêlée against many. In this way,

---

[12] *Kadōsha* (adherents of the Way of verse).

[13] *Tanka*, or a 31-syllable Japanese poem.

[14] This was an era in which schools known as ryūha existed not only for the martial arts such a s archery or swordsmanship but also civil arts. Collectively now they are referred to as *geidō*, or literally the "Way of arts."

[15] Literally, the "two ways of literature and military," this ideal indicates that the warrior should be familiar with the genteel arts and scholarship as well as the martial arts, in other words "The Brush and Sword in Accord."

[16] Outcasts and those on the periphery of society, known as *eta-hinin*.

[17] Acceptance and preparedness for an honorable death had always been an important element in the warrior ethos but unfounded haughtiness in such matters would lead them down the wrong path. He outlines the difference between warriors and others in the next sentence.

he claims honor and distinction for his lord and for himself.[18] This is achieved through superior strength in combat.

There are naysayers in the world at large who claim that studying the Way of combat strategy is futile when confronted with the reality of battle. In response to this claim, I teach that the warrior must practice his craft in such a way that it is practical and functional in all things and at all times, for this is the true Way of combat strategy.

(1) About the Way of Combat[19] (一、兵法の道と云事)

In China and Japan,[20] adherents of this Way are referred to as "masters of strategy." It is inconceivable for a samurai not to study this path.

In recent years, many making their way in the world as "strategists" are, in fact, exclusively engaged in swordsmanship. It was not long ago that, declaring a bequeathal of knowledge from the deities, custodians of the shrines of Kashima and Katori in the province of Hitachi created schools based on divine teachings and taught people throughout the provinces.[21] In times long since gone, there existed what were known

---

[18] An honorable reputation was essential in warrior society. A samurai was nothing without his honor. Dying for one's lord, for example, is a common theme throughout the *Hagakure*. Musashi does not dwell on this point however as he was rarely exclusively in any one lord's service.

[19] In the following I have chosen to number each article sequentially. The traditional Japanese method for marking separate articles is with the ideogram for "1" (一).

[20] A common expression in Musashi's time meaning "everywhere." (Uozumi, Ibid., p. 76)

[21] This is a reference to Tsukahara Bokuden, who first learned the Kashima Shintō-ryū and attracted many students as he journeyed around the country. Musashi's first opponent, Arima Kihei, was a student of Bokuden's school. (Ibid.)

as the "Ten Skills and Seven Arts."[22] Strategy falls under the rubric of "Art," albeit one that is pragmatic. Being practical, this means that it is not limited to the ambit of sword work. It is impossible to understand swordsmanship based on the principles of the sword alone. Naturally, teaching only swordsmanship will not measure up to the laws of combat [in pitched battle].

Looking at the world, I see how people peddle their arts. In addition to the various utensils of their craft, they even think of themselves as commodities for sale.[23] This is analogous to a flower and its fruit, where the fruit is, in fact, much smaller [and is more show than substance]. In any case, colorful displays of technique are flaunted in these martial art "Ways" to force the flower into bloom. Profiteers blathering over this dojo or that dojo,[24] teaching one Way or learning another in the hope of conquering in the fray, fit the [popular] adage "Unripe martial arts are the root of serious harm." Never a truer word has been said.

On the whole, there are four paths that can be traversed in life: the four Ways of the samurai, farmer, artisan and merchant.[25] First is the Way of the farmer. The cultivator arranges various tools and spends the year from spring through

---

[22] Musashi probably used the term generically in reference to various martial arts. (Ibid., p. 77)

[23] As professional teachers in domains.

[24] The burgeoning of dojo, originally a Buddhist term (literally, places where the Way is studied) coincided with the commodification of the martial arts and the proliferation martial art salons patronized by those who had never actually experienced battle but sought certification in one school or another as proof that they were maintaining military preparedness in a time of peace.

[25] From around the seventeenth century, Japanese society was loosely divided into the four classes of warrior (gentry), farmer, artisan and merchant (shi-nō-kō-shō). Musashi does not keep to this order in his explanation.

to fall keeping a keen eye on seasonal changes. This is the Way of the farmer.

Second is the Way of the merchant. The brewer of rice wine acquires various materials to ferment his *sake* and makes his way through life procuring commercial gain contingent on the good or bad quality of his wares. Merchants seek to generate profit to live prosperously. This is the Way of the merchant.

Third is the Way of the samurai.[26] It is called the warrior's Way because the samurai fashions his own tools and knows the intrinsic virtues of his weapons.[27] Is it not a mark of inexperience for a samurai to be oblivious to the merits of his arms because he played no part in their production?[28]

Fourth is the Way of the artisan. The carpenter in his Way has many different tools at his disposal and understands how to use each one. Employing his measure to follow charts with precision as he builds, he applies his skills industriously throughout his life. These are the four Ways of the samurai, the farmer, the artisan and the merchant.

The Way of combat strategy can be likened to the craft of carpentry. Comparing samurai with carpenters is related to the subject of "houses."[29] We speak of noble houses, warrior houses and the "Four Houses."[30] We also talk of the collapse or

---

[26] *Shi* is sometimes translated as "gentry" or "gentleman scholar" but can also be read as "samurai."

[27] Musashi elaborates on this in Article 7.

[28] Musashi was known for his handiwork in producing wooden swords, *tsuba* (ornate hand-guards for swords) and even saddle (Uozumi, Ibid., p. 78)

[29] The *ie* (家) (clan, family or household) was the primary unit of Japanese social organization. It can also simply mean a physical house. Blood kin will form the nucleus of an *ie* in the familial sense, but will also include distant relatives or even non-relatives in its extended network.

[30] A reference to the ancient noble families of the Minamoto, Taira, Fujiwara and Tachibana. Many warriors could (or claimed to) trace their lineage back to one of these four powerful aristocratic families who came to prominence during the Heian period (794–1185). Musashi proudly links his ancestry

continuation of a house. In the arts we refer to a school or tradition as a house. It is because the label "house" is employed as such that I draw parallels with the carpenter's Way. The word "carpenter" (*dai-ku*) is written with the two ideograms meaning "great" and "craft." The Way of combat strategy is also a "great craft," which is why I relate it to the carpenter's endowments. Study the content of these scrolls carefully if you seek to become accomplished in the craft of war. Train assiduously, with the teacher serving as the needle and the student as the thread.[31]

(2) The Way of Combat Strategy—A Comparison with Carpentry (一、兵法の道、大工にたとへたる事)

A general, like a chief carpenter, must bear in mind the laws of the realm, ascertain the statutes of his province and know the rules of his house. This is the "Way of the chief."[32] The chief carpenter remembers measurements for pagodas and temple halls, knows construction plans for palaces and watchtowers

---

with the Fujiwara clan. Another less likely theory about the "Four Houses" is that it refers to the four prevalent schools of the tea ceremony: Ura Senke, Omote Senke, Musha-no-Kōji and Yabunouchi.

[31] A phrase that indicates the traditional Japanese master–disciple relationship. The master leads like a needle piercing the cloth and the disciple follows obediently as he is pulled through unfamiliar terrain (Uozumi, Ibid., p. 78).

[32] The word Musashi uses here is *tōryō*. Within the context of samurai society, *tōryō* meant leader or commander but was also a term used in construction for a foreman or master builder. Construction projects burgeoned as society stabilized during the early part of the Edo period. *Daimyō* set about building majestic castles as the centerpiece of their domains, and bustling townships expanded around them. Carpenters belonged to a highly valued profession. Musashi himself was even appointed to help design the township around Himeji Castle, and he clearly admired the master builders whom he worked with.

and designates tasks to his men to ensure the project is completed. In this way, there are similarities between the chief carpenter and the head warrior.

The carpenter chooses what kind of wood is suitable for building a house. Straight timber without nodes that is pleasing to look at is reserved for the exterior pillars. For the rear pillars, lumber that is straight and strong can be used even if it has knots. Wood of the finest unblemished appearance is suitable for lower and upper rails, doors and sliding panels, even if it is slightly fragile. If the degree of durability needed in different parts of the house is carefully gauged and wood quality is selected accordingly, even a house that is constructed with gnarled, twisted timber will last for years without falling down. Wood that is knotty, warped and weak should be earmarked for scaffolding and kindling when the job is done.

The master carpenter knows who of his men are high, middle or low in terms of ability and delegates jobs that match their capabilities. Some will be tasked with making the alcoves, others the sliding screens, the lower and upper rails, ceiling work, and so on. Those lacking in skill will be deployed to lay the joists, and those with even less aptitude will be kept busy doing menial chores, such as making wedges. Work is sure to progress expediently and economically by properly discerning the competencies of one's men. Things must proceed with efficiency to make headway. One must be unforgiving of shoddiness, cognizant of what is important and aware of the upper, middle and lower levels of liveliness in one's men. One must also be able to energize momentum in the project and know limitations. These are all things the master builder sets his mind to. The principles of strategy and combat are the same.

(3) The Way of Combat Strategy (一、兵法の道)

A trooper is like a regular carpenter. A regular carpenter keeps his tools sharpened, makes his own auxiliary tools and transports them all in his toolbox. Following the master builder's directives, he hews the pillars and beams with his ax, smoothens floorboards and shelves with his plane, shapes openwork and carves intricate ornamentations. Dutifully keeping to the schematics for every nook and cranny, he assembles even the long-roofed passageways to perfection.[33] This is the carpenter's mandate. When a regular carpenter has learned the skills of his trade well and has absorbed the art of planning construction, he too will become a master builder.

A carpenter must have hand tools that cut well. It is important to sharpen them whenever there is a spare moment. With these tools, he expertly fashions cabinets, bookshelves, desks, lamp stands, chopping boards and even pot lids. A trooper has many qualities in common. This requires careful examination. It is imperative that the carpenter ensures that the wood he uses does not warp, the joins are aligned and the boards are planed meticulously so that they do not need to be rasped or manipulated later. This is key. Those who desire to learn the Way [of combat strategy] must take each detail contained within these scrolls to heart, scrutinizing them carefully.

(4) About This Book of Combat—The Five Scrolls (一、此兵法の書、五巻に仕立る事)

This treatise is divided into five Ways. The quintessence for each Way is conveyed in five scrolls: Earth, Water, Fire, Wind and Ether.

---

[33] External corridors (*mendō*) through which horses could be ridden. This may be a play on words by Musashi as *mendō* also means "troublesome."

In the Earth Scroll, I outline the gist of combat from the standpoint of my school. It is impossible to comprehend the true Way through swordsmanship alone. The expert learns "big things" first and then the smaller details, passing from shallow ground through to the deepest sphere of understanding. To first acquire a firm grounding in the direct and correct Way, I call the opening scroll that of "Earth."

Second is the Water Scroll. The attributes of water represent the essence of the mind. Be a container square or round, water adjusts its form to fit the shape of the container. Water may be a small drop or a great ocean. [The deepest] Water has a sparkling hue of emerald green. I present my school in this scroll inspired by the purity of water. Through mastering the principles of sword work, the ability to triumph at will over one man means that you can defeat any man [or number of men] in the world. The mindset for defeating one man is the same as for beating one thousand or ten thousand. The strategy exercised by the general is to modify small-scale matters and apply them on a large scale, much like erecting a giant Buddha statue from a small 12-inch model. It is not easy to write about such things in detail, but the principle underlying strategy is "To know ten thousand things from knowing one thing." With this consideration, I explain the substance of my school in the Water Scroll.

Third is the Fire Scroll. In this scroll I write about combat. Fire becomes big or small and epitomizes a mind of heated ferocity. That is why I write war in this scroll. The Way of war, be it one-on-one combat (small-scale) or a clash of ten thousand versus ten thousand men (large-scale), is the same for all. How to make the mind "think big" or "think small" should be considered judiciously. Big things are easy to see whereas small things are not. In specific terms, with a large body of men it is a challenging task to change tactics at a moment's notice. An individual, however, being of single mind, can alter his approach rapidly. This is what is meant by "small things being difficult to grasp." Ponder this matter carefully. What I write in the Fire Scroll are of things that transpire in an instant. Therefore, it is critical in combat training that the warrior accustoms himself to always maintaining a steadfast spirit. Accordingly, in the Fire Scroll I expound on matters concerning war and dueling.

Fourth is the Wind Scroll. It is titled "Wind" as I do not talk about my school but of the strategy and approaches of other schools.[34] "Wind" is a term that denotes such things as "old trends," "current trends" and "trends of such-and-such a house." In the Wind Scroll I disclose specifics of strategy systems and techniques employed by other schools. It is difficult to understand the self without being acquainted with the customs of others.

In the practice of all Ways and arts, there is such a thing as a wayward spirit. You may believe that you are practicing your discipline conscientiously and are on the right path, but you will deviate from the true Way if your mind wanders. Departure from the truth becomes apparent when observed from the straight path. If you flounder in your pursuit of the true Way and your mind wanders even a little, this will lead to a colossal deviation. Too much of something is just as bad as not enough. This requires close examination.

Other schools of strategy are thought of as mainly embracing the art of swordsmanship. This is an accurate summation. The principles and techniques in my school have completely different implications. The Wind Scroll describes

---

[34] "Wind" (*fū* or *kaze*) not only means the movement of air in the meteorological sense but also implies past or current trends. This is the reason Musashi uses it here, to explain the various idiosyncrasies and patterns seen in schools of swordsmanship.

in detail the features of other schools to inform you of existing trends in strategy.

The fifth is the Ether Scroll. Although I call it the Ether, how can its depth and point of entrance be discerned when it is indicating emptiness? Having comprehended the truth of the Way, you can then let it go. You will find liberation in the Way of combat strategy and naturally attain a marvelous capacity to know the most rational rhythm for every moment. Your strike will manifest on its own, and hit the target on its own. All this represents the Way of the Ether. In the Ether Scroll I write of how one can spontaneously penetrate the true Way.

(5) About This School—Naming it "Nitō"
(一、此一流、二刀と名付る事)

The reason why it is called "Nitō" is because all warriors, from general to rank-and-file, are duty bound to wear two swords in their belts. In days long gone, these swords were called *tachi* and *katana*. Now they are *katana* and *wakizashi*.[35] It goes without saying that the warrior is never without his two swords. Whether he knows how to use them or not is another matter;

---

[35] Japanese swords are collectively referred to as *katana* these days, but original nomenclature for the weapon indicated differences in shape and length. The *tachi* had a single-edged curved blade measuring over 35 inches. The *katana* was shorter at 24–35 inches. With the *tachi*, a warrior would cut (*kiru*) or strike (*utsu*) his enemy, but with the *katana* he would stab (*sasu*) or thrust (*tsuku*). In other words, early references to the *katana* (*uchi-gatana*) show that it served as a kind of dirk for combat at close quarters. However, by the fourteenth century the *katana* was lengthened and eventually replaced the *tachi* altogether as the standard bladed weapon. From this time on, the *katana* was used both as a cutting and thrusting weapon. An even shorter weapon, now referred to as the *wakizashi*, was also combined with the *katana*, but inserted through the sash, to complete the two-sword set. Musashi uses these terms interchangeably throughout the text. To avoid confusion, I use the terms "long sword" and "short sword."

but having two swords at his side is emblematic of the path of the warrior. I call my school Nitō Ichi-ryū (The School of Two Swords as One) to make known the merits of carrying two swords.

The *yari* (pike) and the *naginata* (glaive) are called "spare weapons" but they still belong in the warrior's arsenal. In the Way of my school, it is proper procedure for novices to train by wielding a long sword in one hand and a short sword in the other. This is crucial. When the time comes to abandon life in combat, a warrior must make full use of all the weapons at his disposal. To perish with a weapon uselessly sheathed at one's side is shameful.

Still, it is difficult to manipulate swords freely from side to side with one in each hand. The purpose of practicing Nitō is to get accustomed to using the long sword with one hand. It is standard for bigger weapons such as *yari* or *naginata* to be plied with both hands but long and short swords can most certainly be wielded with one.

It is risky to use one's sword with both hands. You are at a disadvantage when fighting from horseback or when engaged in combat on the run, whether in swamps and muddy rice fields, on stony ground and steep paths, or in the middle of a free-for-all. If you must carry a bow, pike (*yari*), or another weapon in your left hand, your right hand is needed to brandish your sword. That is why it is incorrect in the true Way to hold your sword with both hands. If it is too difficult to dispatch your enemy with a one-handed blow, you can resort to using both at that point. It is not such a difficult matter to comprehend.

First, we learn to simultaneously wield both swords in Nitō and become accustomed to handling the long sword freely with one hand. In the beginning, it is challenging for everyone to brandish a heavy long sword with one hand. Everything is difficult at first—the bow is hard to draw and the *naginata* is awkward to flail. Whatever the weapon, you learn to draw a strong bow as your strength increases for the task, and a sword becomes easier to swing as you become attuned to it through training. The discipline of the sword is not predicated on swiftness in the strike. I will explain this next in the Water Scroll. The basic principle to remember in this Way is that the long sword is employed in open areas and the short sword in confined spaces. In my school, victory must be attainable equally with both long and short weapons. That is why I have no established length for the swords we use. The Way of my school is to win no matter what.

The time when it is better to utilize two swords instead of one becomes evident when fighting single-handedly against multiple foes or when you are battling in an enclosed space. I will refrain from explaining this in detail here. Suffice to say, you need to understand ten thousand things by knowing just one thing well. When you practice the Way of combat strategy, let nothing go unseen. Reflect on this closely.

(6) Knowing the Principles Behind the Two Ideograms in "Hei-hō" （一、兵法二つの字の利を知る事）

In this Way, experts in sword work are conventionally known as "strategists." In the Way of martial arts, those who are skilled in the bow are called bowmen, those who can shoot guns are called gunners, those who carry pikes (*yari*) are called pikesmen and men who wield glaives (*naginata*) are glaivesmen. However, those who specialize in swords are not called long or short swordsmen. Bows, guns, pikes and glaives are all weapons in the warrior's repertoire and so belong in the Way of combat strategy, but there is a reason why swordsmanship itself is identified as "strategy." The origins of strategy are found in the sword. It is through the virtue of the sword that the world is governed and the warrior disciplines himself. One who embodies the virtue of the sword will single-handedly be able to defeat ten adversaries. Just as one man can topple ten men, one hundred can defeat one thousand and one thousand can beat ten thousand. Thus, in my school of strategy one man is the same as ten thousand, which is why I say that strategy encompasses all facets of the warrior's Way.

When addressing the Way, the warrior's path is different from those of Confucianists, Buddhists, tea masters, protocol experts and dancers. Nevertheless, different though these Ways may be, to know one Way in the broad sense means you will find commonality in all of them. It is important for all men to perfect their own Ways.

(7) Knowing the Advantages of Weapons in Combat
(一、兵法に武具の利を知ると云事)

If you know the benefits of different weapons used in battle, you will be able to employ each to optimum effect when the occasion arises. The short sword is best used in a confined area or when close to the enemy. The long sword is generally useful in all situations. On the battlefield, the *naginata* is slightly inferior to the *yari*. The *yari* is useful for taking the initiative, whereas the *naginata* is more suited for making the second move. If two practitioners with equivalent experience were to face off, the one with the *yari* will prove slightly stronger. Depending on the circumstances, however, both the *yari* and the *naginata* will not be particularly advantageous in cramped areas. Nor will they be useful against an enemy under siege in a house [and vice versa]. Best employed on the battlefield, they are principally weapons for pitched battle. However, they will not be of much use if one forgets the Way and studies them as indoor weapons with intricate techniques.

As for bows, they are suitable in tactical maneuvering against an enemy in battle. Because arrows can be released in rapid succession, bows are particularly effective if deployed alongside a detachment of pikesmen or units with other weapons when engaging the enemy on an open battlefield. Notwithstanding, bows are ineffective when attacking forts or assailing an enemy over forty yards away. Nowadays, it goes without saying for archery, and indeed for all the arts, that there are many flowers but not a lot of fruit.[36] Such "arts" are of no use when they are really needed.

Guns rule supreme when fighting from inside a castle. The gun also has many advantages in the field of battle before a clash commences. When the battle is in full swing, however, guns lose their effectiveness. One of the merits of arrows is that their trajectory can be seen as they fly through the air. On the other hand, a bullet fired from a gun is not visible and this is a downside.[37] Consider this carefully.

With horses, it is important that they are responsive to the handling of the reins and have no bad habits. For all implements of war, choose horses that are strong for walking, long and short swords that are sharp for cutting, *yari* and *naginata* that are sharply pointed for stabbing, and bows and guns that

---

[36] Again, Musashi is criticizing the ostentatious but hardly pragmatic nature of various martial art schools that were proliferating in his era. The ideogram that he uses for "fruit" (実) can also be interpreted as "sincerity."

[37] Considering the destructive power of firearms in battle with a range of around 220 yards, it may seem odd that Musashi would be concerned with whether the musket ball could be seen or not. This was a consideration for warriors, however, whose reputations and honor were augmented through their military feats. How many enemy heads a warrior claimed in battle decided the rewards reaped in victory. With musket balls, nobody could be sure who a kill should be attributed to (Uozumi, Ibid., p. 90). It was a reason why guns were eschewed as the dominion of lower-ranked warriors.

are sturdy and will not break when used.[38] The warrior should avoid harboring a preference for any given weapon. Too much of one thing is just as bad as not enough. Do not imitate what others are using. Instead, take to hand weapons that are suited to you and feel right. For both generals and rank-and-file, it is harmful to entertain a strong preference for certain things. Having alternative plans is critical.

(8) About Cadence in Strategy (一、兵法の拍子の事)

All things have their own rhythm. In the case of combat, cadence cannot be mastered without substantial practice. Rhythm is evident everywhere in the world. In the Way of Noh dance, minstrels with their wind and string instruments all have their own harmonious, regular rhythms. In the Way of martial arts, releasing an arrow, firing a gun and even riding a horse have distinctive cadences. Rhythm must never be contravened in any of the arts. Rhythm is also present in things that are invisible. For the samurai, there is rhythm in how he succeeds in service or falls from grace. There is rhythm for harmony and rhythm for discord. In the Way of commerce, there is cadence in the accumulation of great wealth and a rhythm for losing it. Each Way has its own rhythm. Judge carefully the rhythms signifying prosperity and those that spell regression.

There are myriad rhythms in strategy. First, the warrior must know the cadence of harmony and then learn that of discord. He must know the striking, interval and counter cadences that manifest among big and small, fast and slow rhythms [between attacks]. In combat, it is critical for success to know how to adopt the "counter rhythm." You must calcu-

---

[38] Bows and guns, as with swords, were known to break frequently in battle, so bow makers and gunsmiths often accompanied armies in campaigns.

late the cadences of various enemies and employ a rhythm that is unexpected to them. Use your wisdom to detect and strike concealed cadences to seize victory. I devote much explanation to the question of cadence in all the scrolls. Consider what I record and train assiduously.

As written above, your spirit will naturally expand through training diligently from morning to night in the Way of my school's combat strategy. I hereby convey to the world for the first time in writing my strategy for collective and individual combat in the five scrolls of Ground, Water, Fire, Wind and Ether.

For those who care to learn my principles of combat strategy, follow these rules in observing the Way:

1. Think never to veer from the Way
2. Train unremittingly in the Way
3. Acquaint yourself with all arts
4. Know the Ways of all vocations
5. Discern the truth in all things
6. See the intrinsic worth in all things
7. Perceive and know what cannot be seen with the eyes
8. Pay attention even to trifles
9. Do not engage in superfluous activities

Train in the Way of combat strategy keeping these basic principles in mind. Particularly in this Way, inability to comprehensively see the most fundamental matters will make it difficult to excel. If you learn these principles successfully, however, you will not lose to twenty or even thirty foes. First, by dedicating your energies wholeheartedly to learning swordsmanship and practicing the "Direct Way," you will defeat men through superior technique, and even beat them just by looking with your eyes. Your body will learn to move freely through the rigors of arduous training and you will also over-come your opponent physically. Furthermore, with your spirit attuned to the Way you will triumph over the enemy with your mind. Having come so far, how can you be beaten by anyone?

In the case of large-scale strategy [implemented by gener-als, victory is had in many forms]: win at having men of excel-lence, win at maneuvering large numbers of men [effectively], win at conducting oneself properly, win at governance, win at nourishing the people, and win at conducting the laws of the world the way they are meant to be. Irrespective of the Way, knowing how not to lose to others and establishing yourself in name and stature is paramount. This is precisely what the Way of Combat Strategy is.

Twelfth Day of the Fifth Month, Shōhō 2 (1645)[39]
Shinmen Musashi Genshin
[To] Terao Magonojō

---

[39] This date falls one week before Musashi's passing and is thought to be the day in which he handed the manuscript to his disciple, Terao Magonojō. (Uozumi, Ibid., p. 94)

The Water Scroll

Sui-no-Maki

水の巻

Main Points

* *Musashi explains the psychological basis for swordsmanship.*

* *The fundamental elements of combat, such as gaze, posture and how to grip the sword, are described.*

* *The "five combat stances" (kamae) and "five external forms" (kata) that Musashi developed for the Niten Ichi-ryū are introduced.*

* *Musashi delves into the importance of the principles and "pathway" for sword usage and cutting.*

* *Based on extensive combat experience, Musashi gives details of the core techniques, cadences and striking opportunities in his school.*

* *Musashi teaches how to wage combat against several opponents at once.*

* *Translation source is Uozumi Takashi's* Teihon Gorin-no-sho, *pp. 95-123.*

Introduction

The essence of my Niten Ichi-ryū is predicated on the properties of water. As such, in the Water Scroll I explain how to enact the pragmatic principles for sword usage in my school.

It is difficult to express in writing the intricacies of this Way in the manner I would like. Even if words are insufficient, careful contemplation should heighten an intuitive understanding of the principles I am trying to convey. Take time to read this scroll and reflect on each and every word. Inattention to detail will result in many oversights in your appreciation of the path. Although the principles I outlay here are explained from the perspective of individual combat, it is important that they be interpreted as equally pertinent to battles between armies of ten thousand men. What differentiates this Way from others is the intrinsic risk that an error of judgment or moment of confusion will plunge you into bad habits.

Simply reading these scrolls will not lead you to mastery in the Way of combat strategy. Even though the concepts espoused here were written specially for you, do not think it is a matter of simply reading, learning or emulating my instructions. Think of the principles as emanating from within your own heart, and study hard to devise ways of embodying them at all times.

(1) About the Mindset of Combat (一、兵法心持の事)

The mindset in the Way of combat must be no different from one's normal state of mind. In the course of your daily life, and when engaged in strategy, there should be no change whatsoever in your outlook. Your mind should be expansive and direct, devoid of tension, but not at all casual. Keep your mind centered, not leaning too much to one side, swaying serenely and freely so that it does not come to a standstill in moments of change. Consider this carefully.

The mind is not static even in times of calm. In times of haste, the mind does not rush. The body does not carry the mind and the mind does not carry the body. The mind should be vigilant when the body is exposed. The mind must not be absent nor be excessive. Both the high-spirited mind and the lethargic mind are signs of weakness. When the mind's exterior is weak, its interior must be strong so that the enemy cannot gauge your condition. A small man should be aware of the spirit of a larger man and a large man must know the mind of a small man.[1] Both big and small must keep their minds straight and not become trapped by preconceived notions of size.[2]

Be sure to maintain a spirit that is untainted and extensive. Wisdom will settle in the seat of a broad mind. It is crucial to enrich your mind and your wisdom. By enhancing your wisdom, you will be able to sense what is reasonable and unreasonable in the world and will learn the difference between good and evil. You can then see commonality in the Ways of different arts and you will not be open to deception. This is when one can be said to possess the wisdom of strategy in one's heart. Wisdom that is fundamental to the Way of combat strategy is distinctive. When you face adversity in the midst of battle and find yourself completely engaged, never forget to focus your mind on the principles of strategy as this will create within you a steadfast spirit. Study this carefully.

(2) About Posture in Strategy (一、兵法の身なりの事)

With posture, it is important to keep your face neither tilted

---

[1] This can also be interpreted as both small and large numbers of men.

[2] Musashi is warning against the tendency for big men to rely on their strength and small men to depend on speed (Uozumi, Ibid., p. 97).

up nor down, nor leaning to one side, nor grimacing. Your eyes should be composed and your forehead free of furrows. Wrinkles should be confined to the area between your brows. Your eyes should not roll nor blink and your eyelids should be narrowed slightly, taking in a broad view of the surroundings. The line of your head and nose should be straight, with the chin protruding slightly. The neck is upright with the nape tensed, shoulders lowered, back straight, backside in, and with the feeling that your whole body from the shoulders down is a solid entity. Push down from the back of your knees to the tips of your toes and thrust your abdomen slightly forward so that your lower back does not stoop. Insert the scabbard of the short sword into your sash, pressing it against your stomach, keeping it, as they say, "wedged in tight."

With all martial art postures, it is essential to maintain a combat posture in your everyday life and an everyday posture in combat. Study this well.

(3) About the Gaze in Strategy (一、兵法の目付と云事)

One's gaze should be expansive and far-reaching. This is the dual gaze of "looking in" (*kan*) and "looking at" (*ken*). The gaze for "looking in" is intense whereas that for "looking at" is gentle. It is of utmost importance for a warrior to see distant things as if they were close and close things as if they were distant. The warrior must know the enemy's sword without even seeing it. This is critical in combat and must be practiced attentively. Be it in small-scale combat or large-scale battle, one's gaze should be the same. It is vital to be able to see both sides without needing to move your eyes.

It will be impossible to accomplish this method of observing things during the tumult of a fight without conscientious training. Take time to thoroughly study what I have written here. Continually employ this mode of observation in your daily life so that you can apply it in any situation. Examine this carefully.

(4) About Gripping the Sword (一、太刀の持やうの事)

To grip the sword, clasp the hilt loosely with your thumb and forefinger, moderately with the middle finger and tightly with the bottom two fingers. There should be no space between your hands and the hilt. Take hold of your sword with the intention of cutting the enemy.

As you swing your sword down to cut, do not change your grip or allow your hands to tighten. Keep in mind that only the thumb and forefinger are ever so slightly manipulated when slapping, parrying or pressing the enemy's sword. Most importantly, remember to grip the sword with a thought to cutting. The way a sword is gripped is the same in both test cutting[3] and in combat.

Do not allow your hands or sword to become rigid. A rigid hand is a dead hand. A fluid hand is the hand of life. Study this point carefully.

(5) About Footwork (一、足づかいの事)

When moving your feet, raise the tips of your toes slightly so that they float, and kick off strongly from your heels. Depending on the circumstances, move with large or small steps, quickly or slowly, but always in the same way as you would normally walk. There are three styles of footwork that should

---

[3] "Test cutting" was often conducted on cadavers of prisoners to perfect the technique of cutting and precision, and also to evaluate the cutting qualities of a blade.

be avoided. They are known as "jumping feet," "floating feet" and "stomping feet."

The method of alternating footwork is known as *yin-yang*—positive and negative feet—and is fundamental in strategy. This means that you should never move only one foot when cutting, retreating or parrying. Always shuffle right foot-left, right foot-left, one after the other. At no time move with only one foot. Consider this carefully.

(6) About the Five-way Stances (一、五方の構の事)

The five-way stances in swordsmanship are upper (*jōdan*), middle (*chūdan*), lower (*gedan*), left (*hidari-waki*) side and right (*migi-waki*) side. Although there are five stances, their purpose is the same—to cut the enemy. There are no other stances apart from these five. When assuming any of the stances, do not dwell too much on what it is. Think only of cutting the enemy. Whether you take a big or small stance depends entirely on what is best for the situation at hand.

Jōdan position
(Photos of the stances are from the Musashi Monument at the Uganzenji)

Upper, lower and middle stances are fundamental, whereas left- and right-side stances are advanced postures. They are to be used in places that are obstructed overhead or on the flanks. The use of left or right stances should be decided depending on the

Chūdan position

Gedan position

Hidari-waki position (left side)

Migi-waki position (right side)

location. Do not forget that the middle stance is the cornerstone of swordsmanship. It encompasses the essence of all stances. If you look at strategy generally, you will realize that the middle stance is the seat of the general and the other four follow his lead. Understand this notion.

(7) About Sword Pathways (一、太刀の道と云事)

To know the pathway of the sword is to know its true course. To know the pathway means that you can easily wield the sword you always carry with you, even with two fingers. If you try to brandish the sword quickly, it will deviate from the correct trajectory and be difficult to handle. All you need to do is handle the sword in a manner that is calm and collected. If you insist on swinging it briskly, as you would a fan or dagger, this will cause a deviation from the sword's path and you will not be able to control it. An enemy cannot be felled by using a long sword in the same way as hacking frantically with a dagger.

When you cut downwards with a long sword, immediately return it along the same path it came. Likewise, in cutting with a horizontal blow, the sword should return along the same sideward trajectory. Whatever the direction, the sword should be moved widely and vigorously with the arms fully extended. This is the pathway of the sword.

Through mastering the five "exterior sword forms" of my school, your swings will be coherent as the sword's pathway is fixed. Be sure to train diligently.

(8) The Five Exterior Forms—Number One
(一、五つのおもての次第、第一の事)

The first stance is that of the middle. Meet your enemy with the tips of your swords directed at his face. When he unleashes an attack, deflect his blade to the right with your longsword "riding" on top of his. When he redoubles, flip your tip over [assuming the upper stance] and knock his sword down from above holding it there. If he attacks a third time, cut his arms from underneath. This constitutes the first exterior form.

It is impossible to grasp the five exterior forms through simply reading about them. You must embody the movements by actual practice with swords. By attentively studying these five exterior forms, you will grasp your own sword pathway and will learn to deal with all manner of attacks thrown at you by the enemy. Appreciate that there are no other forms in Nitō apart from these five. Be sure to drill yourself in them.[4]

(9) Exterior Form Number Two
(一、おもて第二の次第の事)

The second form involves cutting the enemy with a single blow from the upper stance just as he makes his attack. If he parries your blow, keep your sword at the point of contact and cut upwards from below as he redoubles. Keep cutting this way if he attacks again. When using this approach, know that there are variations in rhythm and mindset. If you practice my school's procedures, you will master the five sword pathways and will win no matter what. Learn them well.

---

[4] Although there are many techniques and procedures studied by adherents of Musashi's school, his point here is that these are the absolute fundamentals. Everything else is an extension or variation of these principles.

(10) Exterior Form Number Three
(一、おもて第三の次第の事)

In the third procedure, assume the lower stance with the tips of your swords pointing down and prepare to strike upward to the enemy's wrists as soon as he launches. He may attempt to deflect and strike your longsword down. In this case, cut his upper arms with a horizontal crosscut, turning the sword to the side with a "traversing cadence" after his strike. When engaging with the enemy from the lower stance, it is essential to stop his strike with a single blow.

When using the swords from the lower stance in accordance with the pathway, you will be able to perceive all when the tempo of the fight is furious or when it is slow. Be sure to train hard with [both] your swords simultaneously.

(11) Exterior Form Number Four
(一、おもて第四の次第の事)

In the fourth procedure, assume the left-side stance and strike at the enemy's hands from underneath as he attacks. If the enemy attempts to strike your sword down, carry through on your upward trajectory to cut at his wrists, extending the swing diagonally up to the height of your shoulders. This is consistent with the pathway of the sword. If your enemy attacks again, parry in line with the sword's path to come in first. This technique requires practice.

(12) Exterior Form Number Five
(一、おもて第五の次第の事)

In the fifth exterior form, the swords are held horizontally in the right-side stance. As the enemy attacks, block [with the short-sword] and swing your longsword up to the upper stance from the low position and follow with a straight downward cut from above. This is essential in learning the pathway of the sword. Mastering this approach will allow you to manipulate heavy swords with ease.

I will not describe in detail the modus operandi of these procedures. Suffice it to say, by exhaustively applying these forms you will learn the Way of sword fighting in my school, master the conventional rhythms of combat, and determine how the enemy uses his sword. Practicing these techniques thoroughly each day and honing your skills in the fray will lead to certain victory, for you will be able to "read" the enemy and know how to exploit the various cadences. Study this well.

(13) The "Stance, No-Stance" Teaching
(一、有構無構のおしへの事)

The teaching of "stance, no-stance" means that you must not focus your mind on assuming a particular fighting stance. Nevertheless, the five stances that I have defined can be utilized as *engarde* postures. With swords in hand, you will adopt various stances as dictated by location and circumstances, such as the posture the enemy is adopting. You must hold the longsword so that you can cut your enemy convincingly at any time. If you assume the upper stance, you can lower your longsword to the middle stance as required. From the middle stance, you can then raise the swords to adopt the upper stance again if the opportunity arises. You can also raise your longsword from the lower stance to the middle stance as needed. Again, depending on the circumstances, bringing the swords to the center from either the left or right sides will generate the lower or middle stance. This is why I teach "There are stances, but there is no stance."

Regardless of the situation, first and foremost the sword is held so that the enemy can be cut.

You deflect your opponent's sword as he attacks, you can parry, slap, strike, stick to or press his sword, but the objective is to cut the enemy. If you become obsessed with the act of parrying, slapping, striking, sticking to or pressing your opponent's weapon, the subsequent strike will lack vigor. Always remember that any stance you assume is for cutting. Practice this well.

As for large-scale strategy, the positioning of soldiers is consistent with the *engarde* stances to ultimately seize victory in battle. It is bad to [inhibit yourself and] settle [on a set stance]. Contemplate this carefully.

(14) About Hitting the Enemy with a "One-Count" Strike (一、敵を打に一拍子の打の事)

The cadence of striking your enemy in "one-count" refers to the action of slashing from the optimal interval for engagement before the enemy is ready to attack. It is executed without revealing any movement before the attack or allowing your mind to become attached to anything. Stop the enemy from acting with the "one-count" strike. Take him with a single blow off the mark before he has time to contemplate drawing his sword, change his stance or launch an attack. This is the "one-count" strike. After perfecting this attacking rhythm, train to beat any opponent with it, then practice exploiting the "pause cadence" where the enemy is momentarily static between phases.

(15) About the "Two-Phase Traversing Cadence" (一、二のこしの拍子の事)

If the enemy parries or retreats as you are about to attack, feint a strike and then follow up with a second real cut just as he relaxes after backing off or parrying the first false attack. This is what is meant by the "two-phase traversing cadence." Just reading about it will not suffice. You will only grasp it when it is taught directly.

(16) About the Strike of "No-Thought No-Form"
(一、無念無相の打と云事)

When you and your opponent attack simultaneously, your body becomes the "striking body" and your mind becomes the "striking mind." As such, your hands will also strike spontaneously with power, speed and no warning. This is the strike of "no-thought no-form" and is of the utmost importance. It is encountered often so must be learned well.

(17) About the "Flowing Water" Strike
(一、流水の打と云事)

The "Flowing Water" strike is employed when the enemy you face quickly tries to back away, disengages his sword or tries to press yours. At this point, inflate your form and spirit, move forward first with your body, then with your sword, and cut him with conviction as if you were enveloping him in torpid water. Understanding this technique will make your strikes incredibly effective. You must have the measure of your enemy to achieve this.

(18) About "Opportunity Knocks" (一、縁のあたりと云事)

As you strike and the enemy counters by blocking or deflecting your blade, capitalize on this opportunity to cut his head, hands and legs. To cut through everything along the line of a single pathway of the sword is what I call "opportunity knocks." Practice this well as it is a method with many applications. Applying this in contests is the only way to master the technicalities.

(19) About the "Flint Spark" Blow
(一、石火のあたりと云事)

The "flint spark" blow is a lightning fast move executed without raising your blade in the slightest. This technique necessitates a swift and sure strike utilizing the legs, body and hands in perfect unison. It is difficult to implement without constant practice. Train assiduously to intensify the speed of the blow.

20) About the "Autumn Leaves" Strike
(一、紅葉の打と云事)

The "autumn leaves" strike entails hitting your enemy's sword down so that he drops it.[5] As the enemy stands before you with his sword poised, smash it down forcefully with "no-thought no-form" or the "flint spark" blow, keeping your sword fixed on his as you follow through. Succumbing to the force, he will inevitably let go of his sword. Drilling yourself in this technique will hone your ability to make the enemy release his sword. Train hard.

(21) About "Body Replaces Sword"
(一、太刀にかわる身と云事)

This can also be expressed as "sword replaces body." When cutting the enemy, the movement of the sword and body are

---

[5] Like leaves falling from the trees in autumn.

generally not unified. Depending on the approach your opponent takes, by maneuvering your body into the attack first, your sword will strike regardless.[6] You can also strike your opponent just with the sword without moving your body at all. It is standard, however, to move your body in to strike, with the sword following. Study this cutting method carefully.

(22) About "Striking and Hitting" （一、打とあたると云事）

Striking your enemy [with the sword] and hitting him are different. A strike must be executed with resolve, no matter what. To hit is essentially probing for prospects. Even if the enemy succumbs to a strong hit, a hit is still a hit. The strike is a conscious effort to cut through. The swordsman must understand this difference. A hit might succeed in slashing the enemy's arms or legs but it must be followed by a decisive strike. A hit is to touch. When you fully understand this notion, the variation between the two will become apparent. Examine the differences.

(23) About the "Body of an Autumn Monkey" （一、しうこうの身と云事）

The "body of an autumn monkey"[7] refers to a procedure in which you do not extend your arms. Encroach into the enemy's space whilst keeping your arms tucked in. Focus on getting as close as possible before executing the strike. Your

---

[6] Analogous to the crack of a whip.

[7] There is some debate as to what the image of an autumn monkey is alluding to. One theory suggests that the monkey wraps itself with its long arms to keep warm in the cool air of fall. Another theory claims that it represents the famous parable of a monkey reaching into a pond of water to grab hold of the moon reflected on its surface, only to lose its balance and fall in.

torso will lag behind if you simply reach out, so try to move your whole body in close as fast as you can, with your hands tucked into your body. It is easy to pounce when you are at arm's length. Study this well.

(24) About the "Body of Lacquer and Glue"
(一、しつかうの身と云事)

The mindset underpinning "body of lacquer and glue" is to advance and attach yourself to the enemy, body to body. Stick steadfastly to the enemy with your head, body and legs. Combatants will often push their head and legs forward but leave their body behind. Attach yourself securely to the enemy, ensuring there are no gaps between your body and his. Consider this well.[8]

(25) About "Contesting Height" (一、たけくらべと云事)

"Contesting height" is to stubbornly infiltrate the enemy's space without shrinking your body in the slightest. As if to contest height, extend your legs, lower back and neck as you raise your face over his and lengthen yourself to assume the superior stature. It is crucial to go forward assertively. Learn this well.[9]

---

[8] Practitioners of modern Kendo might recognize this as akin to *irimi*, or moving the body in close in the last three sets of the Nihon Kendo Kata using the *kodachi* (short sword).

[9] In modern Kendo, this would be similar to *tsubazeriai*, the tussle with *tsuba* (sword guards) adjoined as the protagonists look for a chance to strike a *hiki-waza* (retreating technique).

(26) About "Making it Bind" (一、ねばりをかくると云事)

When you and the enemy strike simultaneously, enter with the sense of binding your swords as he attempts to parry. This is not to hit with too much power but just enough to make the swords stick together firmly. When your sword has fused to the enemy's through the opposition parry, you can then advance with certainty.[10] There is disparity between "binding" and "tangling." Binding the swords is controlling, whereas tangling them is weak. Understand this distinction.

(27) About "Body Smashing" (一、身のあたりと云事)

The instant you penetrate your opponent's space, smash into him with your whole body. Crash your left shoulder into the enemy's chest, turning your head slightly as you do so. Synchronizing your breathing, smash into him vehemently with the aim of rebounding off the impact. Through mastering this technique, you can knock your opponent back ten or twenty feet. The shock will be so great that he may even die from it. Train hard in this procedure.[11]

(28) About the "Three Parries" (一、三つのうけの事)

There are three methods for parrying an attack. First is the "beat parry" in which you deflect the enemy's sword over your right shoulder with a thrust of your long sword directed at his eye. Another method is the "ceding parry" whereby you repel the enemy's sword by thrusting in the direction of his right eye and following through as if to flick his neck. Third, as the en-

---

[10] Imagine the swords stuck together as if they were magnetized.

[11] Again, modern Kendo practitioners will equate this to the *taiatari* movement used to unbalance the opponent.

emy attacks, drive at his face with your left fist as you quickly close in. With this third parry, think of it as delivering a left-handed punch. Drill yourself thoroughly in these techniques.

(29) About "Stabbing the Face" (一、おもてをさすと云事)

When you engage the enemy, it is important to always think of piercing his face with your sword tip. If your mind is committed to stabbing his face, he will feel pressured and will be compelled to withdraw his head and body, causing opportunities to be revealed. Devise ways to master this method. Victory is yours if you have the presence of mind to slide into your opponent. Never forget the importance of what I call "stabbing the face." Train hard to understand this technique.

(30) About "Stabbing the Chest" (一、心をさすと云事)

"Stabbing the chest" is to thrust at the enemy when there are obstacles overhead or at the sides or whenever it is problematic to strike. To avoid the enemy's attack, turn the blade to reveal its back, then recover the tip without incline and counter with a direct stab to his chest. This technique is useful when you are tired or when your blade is dull and not cutting well. Learn how to apply this method.

(31) About "Katsu-Totsu" (一、かつとつと云事)

Katsu-totsu[12] is used when forcing your opponent to retreat or when he tries to counter your attack. Bring your sword up from below as if to stab him. Then, immediately do the op-

---

[12] *Katsu-totsu* is an onomatopoeic term representing a quick succession of cut-thrust, thrust-cut movements.

posite by lowering the sword as if to strike him. The move is executed with a rapid rhythm of stabbing (*katsu*) then cutting (*totsu*). This cadence is encountered often in combat. The compound-riposte of *Katsu-totsu* is executed by raising your sword as if to thrust and then immediately lowering it as if to cut. Practice this cadence repeatedly.

(32) About the "Slapping Parry" (一、はりうけと云事)

The "slapping parry" is used when the exchange of techniques reaches an impasse with a repetitive clang-clang-clang rhythm. Parry the enemy's attack by slapping the side of his blade, followed immediately with a counterattack. Do not put too much force in the slap and do not become distracted by your own parrying. Counter his attack by slapping and then striking in one continuous *stesso-tempo* movement. It is important to take the initiative in both the slapping parry and the following cut. If you capture the right cadence for the slap, your sword will remain true and steady regardless of how powerful the enemy's strike may be. Study this technique well.

(33) About "Dealing to Many Enemies"
(一、多敵のくらいの事)

What I term "dealing to many enemies" is employed when engaging several adversaries at once. Draw your long and short swords and take a broad stance to the left and right as if to fling your foes to either side. Even if they assail you from four directions, push them back as one. Scrutinize the manner with which they attack and deal to them in the order of who comes first. Monitor the entire scenario and simultaneously cut with both swords to the left and right in riposte to their offensive. Pausing after you have struck is perilous. Assume the left and right stances without delay and rile the enemy by fiercely strik-ing each one who is in range. Continuing the drive, cut each in his tracks with the intent of whittling them down.

Herd the enemy back into one place so that they can only attack in single file, like a line of fish strung together. As soon as they are bunched, seize the opportunity to cut through without stopping as you sweep them to each side. You will make little progress if you give them the opportunity to fall into compact groups.

It is also perilous to rely on counter-attacking as this is es-sentially giving the initiative to the enemy. You will win by identifying the attacking rhythm of the enemy and by know-ing where they will come undone. When you can, train against several partners at a time and practice forcing them back. When you understand this method, you will easily be able to deal with ten or twenty adversaries at once. Train hard and investigate ways to master this.

(34) About the "Principles of Engagement" (一、打あいの利の事)

In combat, it is through the "principles of engagement" that victory with the sword is attained. I need not explain the par-ticulars. What is important is to practice conscientiously in order to realize what it takes to win. This is related to sword techniques that represent the true Way of combat strategy, the particulars of which are to be orally transmitted.

(35) About "One Strike" (一、一つの打と云事)

"One strike"[13] is the surest way to victory. It cannot be under-

---

[13] This technique indicates cutting the opponent down with one sword.

stood without a solid grounding in strategy. Training diligently in "one strike" will lead to the embodiment of the combat mind and you will win in any fight. Training is the key.

(36) About "Direct Transmission" (一、直通のくらひと云事)

"Direct transmission" is what I convey to he who has mastered the true Way of the School of Two Swords as One. Temper your body so that it becomes [a weapon for] strategy. Study this well. Other details will be conveyed orally.

This scroll is a summary of the teachings of my school.

To beat people with swords in combat, you must first study the "five external forms" in conjunction with knowing the "five stances" and master the "pathway" of the sword. This way your body will move spontaneously and nimbly. Your mind will perceive the striking rhythms of combat, and the flow of your sword and techniques will be instinctively flawless as you have learned to move unrestrainedly with your body, feet and mind in unison. The principles of strategy will be realized when you defeat one foe or two, and you will come to understand what are strengths and weaknesses in combat. Analyze the content of this scroll article by article as you train and test yourself against various opponents. You will gradually become familiar with the principles of the Way. Be relentless in your study and be patient as you learn the virtue of all phenomena utilizing every opportunity to accumulate actual experience. Engage all and sundry and know their minds. Traverse the thousand-mile road one step at a time. Haste not in your training in the knowledge that this is the warrior's calling. Seek victory today over the self of yesterday. Tomorrow, conquer your shortcomings and then [build] your strong points. Practice all I have written here, mindful of not veering from the path.

Even if you defeat the most daunting of adversaries, if

your victories are not in accord with the principles contained within these scrolls, then they cannot be considered true to the Way. Embracing the principles of the Way, you can prevail over dozens of men. With the accretion of wisdom in sword work, you will master the art of combat for individual duels and large-scale strategy for battle.

One thousand days of training to forge, ten thousand days of training to refine. Be mindful of this.

12th Day of the 5th Month, Shōhō 2 (1645)
Shinmen Musashi Genshin
[To] Terao Magonojō

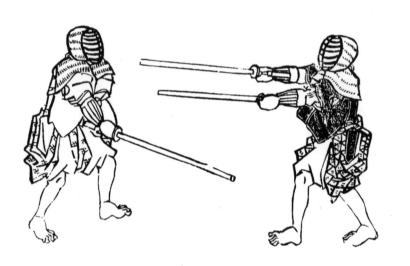

The Fire Scroll
Ka-no-Maki
火 の 巻

Main Points

* *Musashi explains correct positioning to gain an advantage over the enemy.*

* *He introduces the "Three Initiatives" for how to control a fight.*

* *The ability to read the enemy before he can unleash his attack and nipping it in the bud is explained.*

* *Musashi expounds on the importance of observation and using the eyes to "look in" and "look at."*

* *Various psychological tactics to overcome the enemy in mind and body are delved into.*

* *For example, thinking of the enemy as your own troopers and controlling them at will.*

* *He teaches how to identify cracks in the enemy's spirit.*

* *Musashi warns against flogging a dead horse and relying on the same tactics if they are proving ineffective.*

* *Translation source is Uozumi Takashi's* Teihon Gorin-no-sho, *pp. 122-25.*

Introduction

In the Nitō Ichi-ryū I consider battle in terms of fire. I will illuminate matters of strategy and the contest of arms in the Fire Scroll. First, many people think of the principles of strategy in the narrowest sense. Some seek to gain an advantage through subtle manipulation of the four to six inches from the fingertips to the wrist. Or they wave a fan about as they envisage how to win through use of their forearms. Others use bamboo swords and the like to teach how to strike more swiftly through honing agility in their hands and legs.[1] They emphasize gaining even the slightest increase in speed.

In exercising my ideas of strategy, I have put my life on the line many times in combat. I have learned the Way of the sword by risking everything in the divide between life and death. Accordingly, I know the strengths and weaknesses of an enemy's sword as he strikes and have learned how to use the edge and back of the blade [to parry and press]. It is illogical to dwell on small, weak techniques as you prepare yourself to slay an enemy. Small techniques are particularly inappropriate when you are suited in armor [for pitched battle]. It is also not practicable to amass one thousand or ten thousand men for your regular training. You must therefore engage in individual combat to work out the enemy's tactics, to know his strengths, weaknesses and methods, and then to be able to draw on your insights of strategy to beat all and sundry. In this manner you will become a master of the Way. Think to yourself "Who else but I can access the 'direct path'?" and "I will accomplish this in time," then throw yourself wholeheartedly into training in the ways of my school from morning to night. You will find

---

[1] This is most likely a jibe directed at the Yagyū Shinkage-ryū, which employed the bamboo sword (*shinai*) for training since the days of Kamiizumi Ise-no-Kami. This section is a criticism of the growing trend of promoting inconsequential details and form over practicality in swordsmanship.

liberation once you have mastered the skills and will naturally gain a sublime ability pertinent to all things. This is the necessary disposition of a warrior in the art of combat.

(1) About Assessing the Location （一、場の次第と云事）

There is such a thing as "bearing the sun" when assessing the place of combat; that is, to take your stance with the sun at your back. If this is not possible, endeavor to keep the sun to your right-hand side instead [to conceal your long sword]. It is the same when inside a house. Be sure to have the light behind you or to your right if this is not possible. The area to your rear should be free of obstacles, as should the space on your left-hand side. Assume a stance that is restricted on the right [so that the enemy has no space to assail you]. At nighttime also, assume your stance with the same points in mind if your enemy is visible. Take a position with the fire to your rear or with the light to your right. Referred to as "looking down on the enemy," aim to stand at a slightly higher position than your opponent[s]. If inside a house, this means occupying the room's alcove.[2]

As the fight progresses, chase your foe back and try to force him to your left side so that his movement is constrained at the back. Whatever the case, it is vital that you drive him into a tight spot. Continue forcing the enemy back unremittingly so that he does not have time to turn his head and see the precariousness of his position. Inside a house, browbeat the enemy in the same way so that he is impervious to the approaching narrow spaces, such as thresholds, lintels, shutters, sliding doors,

---

2   Musashi advises to stand in the *kamiza*. This literally means "higher seat" and is the decorative alcove (*tokonoma*) found in Japanese-style rooms, which is usually raised a few inches higher than the rest of the floor.

edges and the like. Pushing him back into these obstacles or pillars is the same—he is not to be given respite to grasp his predicament. In all cases, the enemy is grasp into places with bad footing or with barriers to the sides. At all times make use of the location's features and, above all, seek to "win the place." Study this strategy well and train diligently.

(2) About the "Three Initiatives" (一、三つの先と云事)

Of the three initiatives, the first is to initiate the attack before the enemy does. This is called *ken-no-sen*.[3] The second initiative is to attack the enemy after he initiates first. This is called *tai-no-sen*.[4] The third initiative is to attack the enemy as he attacks you. This is called *tai-tai-no-sen*.[5] These are the three initiatives.[6] Regardless of the method of combat, once a fight is underway there are no other initiatives other than these three. Taking the initiative is the key to quick victory and is thus the most crucial aspect of combat strategy. There are many specifics regarding taking the initiative, but it is not necessary to record them in detail here. Victory is only gained through the combat wisdom you possess, taking the appropriate initiative

---

[3] Literally "attacking initiative."

[4] Literally "waiting initiative."

[5] Literally "body-body initiative."

[6] These three timings or initiatives (*sen*) are still taught in modern Japanese martial arts and they determine which techniques can be unleashed. The nomenclature varies but the principles are essentially the same. The first is called *senzen-no-sen* (or *sensen-no-sen*). Just as the opponent's technique is about to take form, you nip it in the bud and defeat it before it can take shape, moving earlier in anticipation of your attacker's intentions. The second is called *senzen-no-sen*. As the opponent sees an opening and attempts to attack, turn it against him with a parry or deflection. *Senzen-no-sen* is also called just *sen*. The third is *go-no-sen*—striking the opponent's attack down or dodging and then counter-attacking immediately as his momentum is compromised.

for each situation and having insight into your enemy's mind.[7]

1. "Ken-no-Sen"—Crackdown Initiative

When you want to attack, keep composed at the start and then suddenly seize the initiative. Take the initiative in an attack with a mind that is fast and furious on the surface but tranquil within. Or advance confidently with a strong spirit and faster footwork than usual and seize the initiative to quickly assail the enemy when you are near him. Another way is to free your mind with the sole intention of routing the enemy from start to finish and win with a spirit brimming with energy. These are all examples of the *ken-no-sen* initiative—cracking down on the enemy before he can hit back.

2. "Tai-no-Sen"—Cleanup Initiative

The second is the "cleanup initiative." As the enemy is about to attack, keep perfectly composed as you present him with a [feigned] sign of weakness. Just as he gets in close, move back resolutely showing that you are about to pounce, and strike him straight and strong as he waivers. This is one way of taking the initiative. Another way is repel him with superior intensity when he moves in to attack. He will then change the cadence of his assault. Capture the instant his rhythm changes and secure victory. These are examples of the *tai-no-sen* initiative—cleaning up after he initiates.

3. "Tai-Tai-no-Sen—Coinciding Initiative

The third is the "coinciding initiative." As the enemy moves in quickly to attack, face him with composure and confidence. As he approaches, suddenly redouble the drive

---

[7] In other words, theory is useless without experience.

of your attack and strike him mightily, snatching victory while he is still plodding. If the enemy advances calmly, be light on your feet and confront him in haste. When he gets in close, finish him off with a powerful strike in consonance with his recoil as you jostle with each other. These are examples of the *tai-tai-no-sen* initiative—coinciding with his attack.

It is difficult to write about such matters in detail. Read what I have outlined here and find ways to work it out for yourself. These three initiatives must be employed in line with to the right time and principles. Although you will not always be the first to attack, seize the initiative to control your opponent's movement.[8] Whatever the case, train diligently to forge a spirit that seeks victory through the application of strategic wisdom.

(3) About "Stopping the Start" (一、枕をおさゆると云事)

"Stopping the start"[9] involves not allowing the enemy's head to rise. In the Way of combat is it perilous to go on the defensive in a bout by allowing yourself to be manipulated. Whatever it takes, you must be the one who dominates. It stands to reason that both you and the enemy are of the same mind, so taking

---

[8] An important point with the "initiatives" Musashi espouses is that in no cases are they reactionary or passive. Even if the enemy initiates an attack, he does so because he is made to. The enemy is lured into initiating an attack and that is used against him.

[9] Musashi uses the term *makura*, which means pillow or head rest, and is usually translated as such, i.e. "Holding Down the Pillow." *Makura* is also used to indicate the introduction or lead-in to a story or piece of music. In the context of this teaching, *makura* is referring to "introduction" or the very beginning of the opponent's technique. The modern Kendo practitioner will recognize this as *debana* or *degashira* techniques.

the initiative and leading him will be difficult unless you can read his intentions. Blocking his attack, deflecting his thrusts and breaking free of his grip means that you are on the back foot in terms of combat strategy.

Through mastery of the correct Way, "stopping the start" involves anticipating your opponent's movements in a fight, knowing what he will do before he knows himself. Stop his strike at the "S…" and do not allow him to continue. This is the mindset of "stopping the start." As he attacks, stop him at the "A…." When he leaps back, stop him at the "L…." When he cuts, nip it in the bud at the "C…." It is all done with the same mind.

Even when the enemy attacks you with some technique, allow futile ones to pass but prevent any that you feel are genuine by not allowing execution. This is foremost in combat. That said, aiming to suppress and thwart your opponent's attempts is akin to losing the initiative. First, any techniques that you employ must be in accordance with the Way.[10] Stifling the enemy's technique at the start just as he contemplates striking, and taking control without giving him a chance to succeed, is the hallmark of a master of strategy, a level attained only through rigorous training. Examine thoroughly the principle of "stopping the start."

(4) About "Traversing Critical Points"
(一、とをこすと云事)

In the context of navigating the ocean, "traversing critical points" entails negotiating difficult currents. There may

---

[10] The techniques must be true to principle and not forced (irrational). Again, in modern Kendo and other martial arts, exponents are still taught to strike "rational" techniques rather than "randomly." In other words, techniques that are the result of a natural progression of events.

be treacherous straits as long as forty of fifty leagues to be crossed, and this is what is meant by "critical points." Traversing problematic positions is also necessary at many junctures during a man's life. With sea routes, you must know the hazardous places that need crossing, know the condition of your vessel and know well the lucky or unlucky omens of each day.[11] Without an accompanying vessel, you must be aware of your position and ride the crosswinds or catch the tailwind. Be prepared for wind changes and to row two or three leagues to port if required. This is how one traverses perilous passages at sea. This mindset relates to overcoming problematic points in life and should be applied with due concern to the demands of the situation.

In swordsmanship and in the midst of pitched battle, the ability to know the right moment to traverse a critical point is essential. Know the enemy's strengths and have a firm grasp of your own capabilities. Traverse the peril at the optimum point just as a worthy mariner navigates ocean routes. Once crossed, the mind becomes tranquil. If you successfully get past the critical point, your opponent will tire, the initiative will be yours and victory is there for the taking. The mind of "traversing critical points" is essential in large-scale strategy as well as individual combat. This must be examined carefully.

(5) About "Knowing the Conditions"
（一、けいきを知ると云事）

"Knowing the conditions" in large-scale battle strategy is to detect if the enemy is flourishing or failing, cognizant of their numbers and intent, taking their location into consideration

---

[11] This can be interpreted as a reference to the weather and also to days of good or bad fortune in accordance with the traditional Japanese calendar.

and carefully scrutinizing the enemy's fettle. With this information at your disposal, direct your own men in accordance with the principles of strategy and claim certain victory through exploiting the initiative.

When engaged in individual combat also, bear in mind the enemy's school and ascertain his strengths and weaknesses. It is important to take the initiative and take advantage of the enemy's state by distinguishing fluctuations and pinpointing the intervals in his rhythm. With superior insight, you will always be able to see the condition of things. When you can move freely in combat, you will see into the enemy's mind and find many ways to win. Use your ingenuity.

(6) About "Trampling the Sword" (一、けんをふむと云事)

"Trampling the sword" is exclusive to combat.

In the case of large-scale strategy, the enemy will start by shooting their bows or harquebuses. It will be difficult to penetrate the enemy line if you attack after they release a volley of arrows and bullets as they will have time to re-draw their arrows and load powder in their barrels. The best way to deal with bows and harquebuses is to storm the enemy as they shoot. By attacking quickly, the enemy will not have time to nook their bows or reload their harquebuses. React rationally to whatever the enemy throws at you and prevail by trampling their maneuvers underfoot.

In the case of man-to-man combat, if you strike after each blow by the opponent, the engagement will become *quid pro quo*. If you trample his sword underfoot, he will be defeated on the first attack and will not have an opportunity to make a second. Trampling should not be limited to the feet. The body is used to trample, the spirit is used to trample and, of course, the sword is used to trample. No respite should be given so that the enemy has no chance to make a second move. This is precisely how you take the initiative in any situation. Move in synchronization with the enemy, not with the intent of colliding with him, but to finish him after the encounter. Be sure to explore this teaching carefully.

(7) About "Recognizing Collapse" (一、くづれを知ると云事)

All things are prone to collapse. Houses collapse, the body collapses and enemies collapse when their time is up. Cadences can become confused and collapse. In large-scale strategy, the enemy must be pursued relentlessly as soon as you sense cracks in their cadence. Allowing the enemy to breathe by not capitalizing on this moment of collapse will give them a chance to recover.

When fighting a single opponent, he may start to collapse when his rhythm becomes muddled. He will bounce back if you are not vigilant and you will make no progress. Just as he is on the verge of collapse, immediately rush at him and attack relentlessly so that he cannot even look up. Charge straight at him with single-minded resolve. Beat him to a pulp so that he has no chance to reorganize. Learn the gravity of smashing the enemy to pieces. If he is not pulverized, his spirit will remain. Examine this well.

(8) About "Becoming your Enemy" (一、敵になると云事)

"Becoming your enemy" is to put yourself in his place. Think of a burglar who is holed up in a house he is attempting to rob. We are prone to overestimating the enemy's strengths. By putting yourself in his position, however, you realize that he must feel that the whole world is against him. With no way out, he is like a pheasant in a cage. The assailant zooming in to kill him is a falcon. Consider this carefully.

Even in large-scale strategy, there is a tendency to think that the enemy force is strong. This leads to a cautious approach. There is little that should concern you if you command plenty of good men and understand the principles of strategy for defeating the enemy. You must also "become your enemy" in individual combat. Defeat comes ahead of the engagement through believing one's foe is a skilled adherent of the Way who exemplifies the principles of strategy. Reflect on this.

(9) About "Releasing the Four Hands"
（一、四手をはなすと云事）

"Releasing the four hands"[12] is a tactic used when you and your opponent are competing with the same mind and have reached an impasse. If you sense that you are battling with the same mind, discard your current methods and employ alternative ones to seize victory.

In the case of large-scale combat, if you engage with the intention of [keeping] "four hands" in play, you will not make progress and your allies will suffer heavy losses. Be ready to change your approach instantly and execute an unexpected tactic to outfox the enemy.

This is true for individual combat, too. If you suspect you are fighting in a "four hands" stalemate, gauge your enemy's frame of mind and win by changing tack and cutting a completely different line of attack. Consider this carefully.

---

[12] Think of two Sumo wrestlers locked in a hold with both hands on each other's *mawashi* belts.

(10) About "Shifting the Shadow"
(一、かげをうごかすと云事)

"Shifting the shadow"[13] is applied when you are unable to fathom the enemy's mind. With large-scale strategy, when you cannot ascertain the enemy's situation, feign the start of an all-out assault. Then their state will become obvious and it will be easy to rout them with the right approach when their tactics have been exposed.

In the case of individual combat, if your opponent assumes a rear or side posture to conceal his intentions, his mind will be revealed through the movement of his sword if you lure him with a feint. Thus, with objective divulged you can snatch victory by utilizing the right approach. You will miss the right rhythm if you are haphazard. Study this thoroughly.

(11) About "Arresting the Shadow"
(一、かげをおさゆると云事)

"Arresting the shadow" is a tactic used when you perceive that the enemy is getting ready to attack.

In large-scale strategy, the moment you recognize that the enemy is about to act, you suppress them. If you convincingly demonstrate your intent to completely stifle their assault, the enemy, being constricted, will quickly have a change of heart. You can then alter your approach to seize the initiative and defeat the enemy at will with a clear mind.

In individual combat, upon sensing the enemy's deter-

---

[13] The ideogram Musashi uses here for "shadow" is 陰. In the following article, he uses a different ideogram, 影. The former is alluding to the concept of *yin* and the latter *yang*, or negative (dark) and positive (light), respectively. In other words, the inference of "shadow" in Article 10 is when you cannot see the enemy's intent (Uozumi, Ibid., p. 137). In Article 11, the opposite is true.

mination to attack, immediately snuff out his drive with an appropriate rhythm. Catch the beat of his retreat. Taking the initiative, defeat him when you sense the right moment. Research this carefully.

(12) About "Infecting" (一、うつらかすと云事)

All things can be infectious. Drowsiness is infectious, as is yawning. Even time is communicable. In large-scale strategy, if you sense that the enemy is agitated and hesitant, pretend not to notice and take your time. Seeing this reaction, the enemy will drop their guard. With your mind set free, attack mercilessly the instant the enemy has been infected by your inaction.

With individual combat, loosen your body and spirit and, as your opponent inadvertently follows suit, seize the initiative to attack powerfully and quickly. There is a similar tactic, "making the enemy drunk." You contaminate his mind by exhibiting listlessness, hesitancy or weakness. Be sure to explore this strategy thoroughly.

(13) About "Eliciting Agitation" (一、むかつかすると云事)

There are many ways in which one can become agitated, such as being within an inch of danger. A second way is when faced with an impossible task. The third way is through surprise. Study this.

In large-scale strategy, it is important to know how to evoke irritation in the enemy. By suddenly assaulting with vim and vigor when they least expect it, and not giving them a chance to recoup, you can seize the initiative and finish them off in their moment of indecision.

For individual combat, trick the enemy by moving slowly at first and then suddenly attack him with force. It is imperative to not let up, crushing him according to the movement of his body and the fluctuations of his mind. Learn this method well.

(14) About "Invoking Fear" (一、おびやかすと云事)

Many things can invoke fear. Fear is aroused when the unexpected happens.

With large-scale strategy, fear can be conjured in the enemy not only by what they see. Fear can be incited by bellowing, making something small seem greater in size, or by unexpectedly assaulting their flank. Victory is gained by taking advantage of the enemy's muddled cadence prompted by a moment of terror.

In the case of individual combat, it is important to beat your opponent by doing something unexpected with your body, sword or voice to startle him. Study this well.

(15) About "Blending" (一、まぶるると云事)

When you clash with the advancing enemy and an impasse has been reached, this is the time to become one with him through "blending." From within the tussle you must find an opportunity to win.

In both large- and small-scale strategy, when the engagement languishes because both are fighting with equal force, blend with the enemy so that it is impossible to make a distinction. From there you can find an opening and to seize victory, winning strongly. Study this tactic in detail.

(16) About "Hitting the Corners" (一、かどにさわると云事)

Pushing through unyielding objects from the front can be an impossible task. In such cases, the tactic of "hitting the corners" is effective. With large-scale strategy, look at the number of opponents before you assault a corner—a protruding area—of their force. If a corner can be reduced, this will affect the entire unit. As one corner is weakened, it is important to then attack other corners in the same way and seize control. In individual combat, even inflicting minor damage on corners of the enemy's body will make him crumble and will lead to victory. Study this carefully and understand the principles needed to win.

(17) About "Causing Confusion" (一、うろめかすと云事)

To "cause confusion" is to make the enemy lose heart.

In large-scale strategy, calculate what is going through the enemy's mind on the battlefield and use your strategic prowess to cause confusion among the opposing troops by making them question "Here or there? This or that? Slowly or quickly?" The enemy is left vulnerable when their rhythm is in disarray.

In individual combat, disorient the opponent by employing various techniques to attack according to the circumstances. You can feign a thrust or strike or get in close. You can easily pick him off once you have identified the confusion infecting his mind. This is indispensable in combat, so study it well.

(18) About "The Three Cries" (一、三つの声と云事)

The "three cries" bellowed before, during and after an encounter are distinctive. The method of shouting depends on the situation. A cry is a vocalization of one's life force. We roar against fires, the wind and the waves. The cry reveals the degree of someone's vitality.

In large-scale strategy, we roar at the enemy with all our

might at the commencement of battle. Vocalizations lower in pitch are emitted from the bottom of the gut in the midst of combat. Then we bellow with gusto in victory. These are what are referred to as the "three cries."

In individual combat, yell *Ei!* while feigning an attack to lure the opponent into making a move, and then follow up with a blow from your sword. Roar to pronounce victory after the enemy has been felled. These are known as the "before-after cries." Do not cry out loudly as you strike with your sword. If you emit a cry during the attack, it should be low in tone and match your cadence. Study this well.

(19) About "Mixing In" (一、まぎるると云事)

What I call "mixing in" is when two armies clash in pitched battle is striking at one of the enemy's strong points. When that point begins to yield, divert the brunt of your attack to another strong point in the enemy force. It is basically alternating the target of your assaults as if zigzagging down a slope.

This is an important tactic when fighting alone against several opponents. Do not try to defeat each side. When the enemy is pushed back in one direction, turn and attack the strongest opponent on the opposite side. Sensing the cadence of your opponents, move as if zigzagging your way down a path from left to right according to their reaction in a rhythm that suits you. After determining the condition of your enemies, disappear among them and strike with no intention whatsoever of pulling back. You will then see countless opportunities to win. This is also valid for getting in close to a strong opponent in individual combat. To mix in, you must be of the mind to not retreating even one step. You must learn what "mixing in" while advancing entails.

(20) About "Crushing" (一、ひしぐと云事)

To "crush" is to see your opponent as weak and yourself as strong and smashing him to bits.

In large-scale strategy, irrespective of their number, the enemy will show their vulnerability if they hesitate or are disoriented. At this point, crush the enemy from the top down. Overwhelm them with a burst of energy as if to push them back and obliterate them. If the crushing blows are insufficient, the enemy may recover. Crush them as if they were in the palm of your hand. Study this well.

In the case of individual combat, if your adversary is not skilled or he backs off because his rhythm is disrupted, he must be crushed immediately and given no chance to breathe or look you in the eye. It is crucial that he is not afforded the slightest opportunity to get back on his feet. Learn this well.

(21) About "The Mountain-Sea Alternation"
(一、さんかいのかわりと云事)

The mind of "mountain-sea"[14] means that it is perilous to execute the same move three times in a fight. It may be unavoidable to employ a tactic twice but never do it three times. If an attack is unsuccessful, keep applying pressure and try again. If it still has no effect, quickly adapt and change your approach. If your next move doesn't work, then try another. The mindset underlying this is when the enemy is thinking of "mountain," attack him as the "sea." If he is thinking "sea," take him down as the "mountain." This is the Way of strategy. Study it exhaustively.

---

[14] This is a play on words by Musashi. *San-kai* (山海) means "mountains and sea." The ideograms 三回, meaning "three times," is also pronounced *san-kai*.

(22) About "Knocking the Bottom Out"
(一、そこをぬくと云事)

What I call "knocking the bottom out" is as follows. You may feel you have succeeded through application of the principles of the Way in battle when, in fact, in his heart the enemy has not yet yielded. On the surface that he is defeated but deep down his spirit is still very much in the fight. When this occurs, replenish your mind and raze the enemy's spirit by ripping it apart so that he is defeated beyond doubt. Take care to confirm this.

"Knocking the bottom out" [of his fighting spirit] can be accomplished by the use of a sword, with the body or with your mind. There is not only one way to achieve this. Once the stuffing has been knocked out of the enemy, there is no need to keep fixed on him. If this is not the case, continue to maintain vigilance. It is difficult to destroy an enemy who still harbors a residual spirit to fight. You must study diligently to understand the meaning of "Knocking the Bottom Out" for both large- and small-scale strategy.

(23) About "Starting Anew" (一、あらたになると云事)

"Starting anew" is a tactic used when you and your opponent are tangled in a deadlock. In such a case, you must rid yourself of prior feelings and start afresh as if doing everything for the first time. This way, you can employ a new cadence and snatch victory. "Starting anew" in a gridlock where you are unable to take the initiative requires an instant change of mind and the execution of an entirely different maneuver to win.

The tactic of "starting anew" is also crucial in large-scale strategy. You will come to see it quickly with knowledge in strategy. Study it well.

(24) About "Rat's Head, Ox's Neck" (一、そとうごしゅと云事)

In "rat's head, ox's neck,"[15] when you and the enemy have become fixated on particulars in the engagement, think of the Way of strategy as being both a rat's head and an ox's neck. When you are fighting with subtleties, suddenly expand your mind and transform into something big. Transitioning between large and small is essential in strategy. It is important for a warrior to have as his standard mindset a "rat's head, ox's neck." This is crucial in both large- and small-scale strategy and should be examined carefully.

(25) About "The General Knows His Troops" (一、しやうそつをしると云事)

"The general knows his troops" is pertinent in all forms of combat. In this Way, if you study relentlessly to build strategic wisdom, you will come to think of the enemy troops as your own and be able to command them to move as you see fit. You will be able to direct at will. You are the general and the enemy are your men. Be sure to master this strategy.

(26) About "Releasing the Hilt" (一、つかをはなすと云事)

"Releasing the hilt" has several implications. It can mean the mind of winning without a sword or the mind of not winning with a sword.[16] The various approaches that stem from this

---

[15] Some copies of *Gorin-no-sho* use the ideogram for horse (午) rather than ox (牛) (Uozumi, Ibid., p. 149). In either case, contrasting the head of a rat with the neck of a strong beast, be it a horse or an ox, is effectively the same thing.

[16] A somewhat cryptic teaching, Musashi is alluding to the idea that the warrior should not be attached to his weapon. He must have an open mind and be able to adapt without inhibition as the situation demands.

mind cannot be written in detail here. Train persistently.

(27) About "The Body of a Boulder"
(一、いわをのみと云事)

One who has mastered the Way of combat strategy can instantaneously become like a boulder. Nothing can touch him and he will be immovable. Details conveyed orally.

I have long pondered the articles logged here about my school of swordsmanship. This is the first time I have put them in writing. As such, I fear that the order is somewhat jumbled and some principles have not been expressed in sufficient detail. Even so, what I have recorded will serve as markers for those dedicated to pursuing this Way.

Since I was a young man, I have devoted my life to studying the Way of combat strategy. I have toughened my body and finessed my skills of sword work, with my knowledge evolving over several stages. I have ventured forth to observe the methods of other schools. Some explain lofty theories while others are concerned with the execution of intricate techniques. Although they exude an air of skillful beauty, they are devoid of the true spirit of strategy. It is possible to garner technical artistry and hone the mind in these arts. Alas, however, training in these disciplines leads to bad habits that block progress in the true path. Once habits are formed, they stick and are almost impossible to remedy. The Way of strategy in its truest manifestation falls into decay and is lost. The principles behind the mastery of swordsmanship and winning in combat are one in the same. If you learn my teachings of strategy and abide by its rules, you need never doubt that victory will be yours.

前權漢堂吳籍書

腰間寶劍截流光
手裏清風都強敵
可惜三軍屬指揮
丹青寫出益深藏

妙解院殿雄五公大居士肖像

Hosokawa Tadatoshi (1586–1641), lord of the Kumamoto domain who was Musashi's patron. Musashi wrote *Heihō 35* at the request of Tadatoshi.

TOP: The five scrolls comprising *Gorin-no-sho*. Traditional documents in Japan were written on individual leaves of *washi* paper and glued sequentially to a thicker paper backing to be rolled up for storage. This set is a reproduction of the Hosokawa Book, an early transcription of Musashi's original manuscript.

ABOVE: Earth scroll interior.

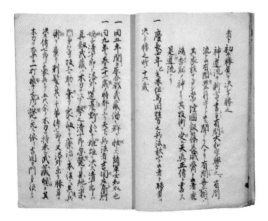

TOP: Novelist Yoshikawa Eiji's classic prewar work of historical adventure fiction, *Miyamoto Musashi*.

ABOVE: Written in 1776 by Toyoda Kagehide, an instructor of Niten Ichi-ryū to Hosokawa domain samurai, *Nitenki* became an influential, albeit flawed, source of information regarding Musashi's life.

Although comparatively rare, there are some practitioners of the modern martial art of Kendo who compete with two swords in the style of Musashi.

ABOVE: Reigandō, meaning "Spirit Rock Cave," is located in the west of Kumamoto prefecture and is where Musashi spent his last years meditating and writing his *Book of Five Rings*.

LEFT: Musashi was not only a talented artist but also an accomplished craftsman. This saddle is attributed to him.

ABOVE: The Musashi Budokan (martial arts hall) was constructed in 2000 in Mimasaka City. Its design was inspired by the iconic "Musashi Tsuba," a sword guard designed by Musashi. The Musashi Budokan hosts many martial art events, including the popular Otsū Cup Women's Kendo Tournament inspired by Musashi's fictional love interest in Yoshikawa Eiji's novel.

RIGHT: This sword guard (*tsuba*) is easily recognized by sword aficionados as the "Musashi Tsuba." Often found on imitation swords today, it was one of many designed by Musashi.

A bronze statue of Musashi (right) about to deliver the death blow to Sasaki Kojirō. The statue, located on Ganryūjima Island, has become one of several popular sites associated with the Musashi tourism industry.

ABOVE: This mid-Edo period painting shows Musashi defeating Kojirō with two swords. Like many depictions of Musashi in various media, it is not historically accurate. Musashi killed Kojirō with a wooden sword that he fashioned especially for the duel.

OPPOSITE: Early copies of the "Revenge on Ganryūjima." This story became an immensely popular play in Kabuki theater from the mid-Edo period.

The Kokura Monument in Tamukeyama Park, Kita Kyushu, was erected in honor of Miyamoto Musashi in 1654 by his adopted son, Iori. There is a monument to Sasaki Kojirō nearby. The Musashi and Kojirō Festival is held annually in April.

余之祖先人王六十二代目顕氏改福田原居于播刕加南郡河南庄米蔭邑子孫世々庶于此馬冒祖田左在京大夫員光祖考曰久光自員光来則相続属于小寺其甲之庵下故於筑前子孫見存于今馬有作刕之顕氏神免者天正之間無嗣而卆于筑前秋月城交遺承家日武蔵掾宏信後改氏宮本亦無子而以余為義子故余今称其氏余比結髪元和之間信別生仕小笠原右近大夫源也政主于播刕明石今又従千豊之小倉也鈇

古新村上新村米蔭中嶋塩市令市総十七邑之氏神義鏡

木村 加古川 西宿村 船本村 友澤村 橋屋村

莆神也而米蔭又別宰菅神影近歳二社共殆頽朽今巳得新二社焉大神之威歳人之得必祐天無一志石謹吾家兄田原吉久舎小原玄昌及田原正久竿伴斬匠焉而今巳得新二社而神護可知矢雖然常人之質實徳未傭如其枸耕統一攀丹析連縦毫不具所謂心誠誠道甚也両則縦雖不析而神護有知矢雖然常人之質實徳未傭如其枸耕統一仰無神人有威通武其玄昌以小原為氏者播刕加郡小原城主上野守藩信利其嗣信先生等一人石無男天正之聞屬播刕三木城主中川右衛門大夫庵下到高巖戦死焉故母輀伴玄昌継其氏云時寛慶二巳卯五月日宮本伊織原真次曰

泊大明神美祿老傳云所奉勸請紀伊日

The wooden tablet discovered in the Tomari Shrine in Kakogawa. The text was written by Musashi's adoptive son, Iori.

An iconic depiction of Musashi in his later years when he lived in Kumamoto.

實
三
學
真

Aoki Kaneie (dates unknown) was an early student of Musashi who created his own school using the sword and *jitte*. He called it Aoki-ryū but later changed it to Tetsujin-ryū (Ironman School). He purportedly had nearly 9,000 students.

"Genso Shinmen Gennosuke-zō." Painted by Tsubaki Chinzan in the early 1800s, it has an inscription that reads "Bennosuke (Musashi) after defeating Arima Kihei in mortal combat aged thirteen." Copied from an earlier portrait, it is, in fact, a depiction of Musashi in his fifties when he was in Nagoya. (Shimada Art Gallery)

"Daruma-zu."
Musashi became an
ardent follower of
Zen and received
the Buddhist name
Niten Dōraku. He
left many paintings
of Hotei and Bod-
hidharma, the Zen
Buddhist patriarch.
This is a depiction
of Bodhidharma.

聖人垂統屬濂翁
秋月明ゝ胸宇中
雲際光風開不閟
春陵門是廣寒宮
　後學林道春謹贊

"Shūmoshuku-zu," Musashi's painting of the influential Chinese Confucian scholar Zhou Dun-yi. A poem at the top of the picture was inscribed by Hayashi Razan, a leading Confucian scholar of the Edo period who was known to Musashi.

Many Musashi movies have been produced in the postwar period. Most of them focus on his adventures up to the duel with Sasaki Kojirō on Ganryūjima, and are largely based on Yoshikawa Eiji's portrayal of his life.

SCROLL 4

The Wind Scroll
Fū-no-Maki
風 の 巻

Main Points

* *In the Wind Scroll Musashi outlines idiosyncrasies he identified in other schools of swordsmanship. The term Fū which means wind is also used to mean things that are trendy or prevalent.*

* *He emphasizes outwitting and overcoming opponents who rely on brute strength, and conversely not to fall into that trap.*

* *He expounds on why relying purely on speed is bad.*

* *Musashi criticizes schools that incorporate too many combat forms and procedures as being superfluous.*

* *The right and wrong ways of teaching combat strategy are described.*

* *Translation source is Uozumi Takashi's* Teihon Gorin-no-sho, *pp. 153–69.*

Introduction

Mastering combat strategy requires studying the Ways of other schools. In the Wind Scroll[1] I outline various traditions of strategy and explain their characteristics. It is difficult to fully comprehend the Way of my school without understanding the other disciplines.

Upon researching other schools, I found some center on executing powerful techniques with extra-long swords. Other schools focus on the use of short swords called *kodachi*. Or they create myriad forms for sword work, conveying the various stances as "exterior" and the Way as "interior" teachings. In this scroll I will show how such schools have veered from the true path of strategy. I will evaluate the strengths and weaknesses of these approaches and elucidate the principles.

The principles of my school are in a class of their own. Other schools extol the virtues of their colorful, flowery techniques like produce peddled to make a living. Is this not a deviation from the true Way?[2] Are not the so-called "strategists" in the world today limiting their training to sword work believing that victory can be had simply through agility and subtle skills for wielding the sword? In either case, this is not the correct Way. I will now list the shortcomings of other schools. Study these well so that you may grasp the logic behind Nitō Ichi-ryū.

---

[1] "Wind" in the context of this scroll means "trends" or "modus operandi" of other schools. Musashi avoids naming the schools but surely his disciples would be aware of what styles of swordsmanship he was alluding to.

[2] There is a negative inference here that the techniques of other schools are ostentatious and without any practical worth other than to make their styles stand out in the hope of gathering more students. This was referred to derisively as *kahō kenpō*, or "flowery sword methods," and became the impetus for the development of full-contact sparring equipment around the beginning of the eighteenth century enabling swordsmen to actually fight each other safely. This is represents the beginning of modern Kendo.

(1) Schools Employing Extra-Long Swords
(一、他流に大きなる太刀を持事)

Some schools prefer to employ extra-long swords. From my perspective, however, these are weak schools. The reason is because they clearly fail to comprehend the principle of winning in any circumstance and think that an extra-long sword will be advantageous for striking the enemy from afar. That is [the only reason] why they prefer a longer sword.

It is said that "even an extra inch gives the upper hand." However, this is a meaningless teaching advocated by those ignorant of combat strategy. With no understanding of the [deeper] principles of strategy, they seek to win from a safer distance with a longer weapon. This is indicative of a weak mind and is why I see that their strategies as being feeble.

If an adherent of such a school were to engage at close quarters with the enemy, the longer the sword, the harder it is to strike with. It cannot be wielded freely and will become burdensome. He will find himself disadvantaged against an enemy employing a short sword or one fighting with his bare hands. Those who prefer extra-long swords no doubt have their reasons but they have no validity when viewed from the perspective of worldly truth. Will a short sword always lose against a long sword? When forced to fight where space is restricted in height and breadth, or when you are in a place where only a short sword is permitted,[3] preference for a long sword will be your undoing as it a cop-out in strategic ability. Moreover, some people lack strength and are not built to wield an extra-long sword. Since ancient times it has been said that "long and short are combined." Therefore, I am not opposed to long swords per se. I do, however, dislike the bias for using longer swords.

---

[3] For example, inside a palace or somebody's house. Long swords were usually not allowed to be worn indoors.

In large-scale strategy, the presence of numerous troops is linked with an extra-long sword. Smaller numbers are consistent with the use of a short one. Is it not viable for a small number of troops to take the fight to a larger force? The virtue of strategy is precisely that smaller numbers can triumph [if guided correctly]. From the earliest days, there are many examples of small forces crushing big armies. In our school, this kind of narrow-minded preconception is to be rejected above all else. Research this well.

(2) About Schools That Use Swords with Force
（一、他流におゐてつよみの太刀と云事）

One should not consider a sword [stroke] in terms of being strong or weak. The cut will be coarse if the sword is brandished with too much brute force. Such an uneven technique will make victory difficult. You will not succeed in cutting through human flesh and bone if you think only of striking with brute force. It is also bad to use too much power when testing the cutting power of a blade (*tameshi-giri*).[4] When punishing some mortal foe, nobody thinks of cutting feebly or brutishly. "Cutting to kill" it is not achieved with a mind to do it strongly, and certainly not weakly. It is achieved with just enough power to ensure death. Your own sword could break into pieces by hitting the enemy's sword with excess strength. Consequently, it is senseless to strike with excessive force.

---

[4] *Tameshi-giri* means "test cutting." Cutting through the cadavers of dead or alive prisoners was a morbid practice in the Edo period to test the cutting quality of a blade and for refining skills in sword usage. The tangs of some Edo-period swords are marked with proof of how many piled-up bodies the sword successfully cut through when tested. *Tameshi-giri* is still practiced today by sword aficionados but using the more agreeable target of rolled up straw mats.

In large-scale strategy, relying on force of numbers to rout the enemy will lead to him countering with equal force. Both sides will be the same. Winning at anything is not achievable if correct principles are ignored. Thus, the underlying principle of my school is to defeat the enemy in any situation by applying strategic wisdom, without incorporating anything that is "excessive."[5] This must be researched attentively.

(3) Schools That Use Short Swords
(一、他流に短き太刀を用る事)

Some warriors try to win using only short swords but this is at variance with the true Way. Since antiquity, swords were called *tachi* and *katana*, proving that distinctions have long been made between short and longer lengths.[6] Warriors of superior strength can brandish a long sword as if it were light and thus there is no reason for them to prefer a shorter sword. They are, in fact, capable of wielding even longer weapons, such as *yari* (pikes) and *naginata* (glaives). With shorter swords, it is ill advised to look for openings as the enemy swings his blade and closing the distance to grab him. Aiming for an opening as the opponent attacks gives the impression of relinquishing the initiative and should be avoided as your swords will become entangled. Moreover, using a shorter sword and jumping in to close the distance or grab the enemy is futile when faced with several opponents. Warriors who have learned to use the short sword try to dispatch several of the enemy with sweeping cuts, jumping in and spinning around. They will end up defending

---

[5] The term Musashi uses here is *muri*. This can mean excessive but also "irrational" or "unreasonable."

[6] *Tachi* were classified as swords over 36 inches (90 cm) in length, and *katana* were 24–36 inches (60–90 cm) (Uozumi, Ibid., p. 157). As such, the *katana* was designated as the short sword.

themselves and falling into disarray as this is not in line with the principles of strategy. Ideally, the way to win with certainty is to drive the enemy flustering them as they dash here and there while you remain upright and strong.

This principle also applies to large-scale strategy. At the core of strategy is subjugate the enemy and precipitously push them back.

If you are accustomed to blocking, evading, disengaging or deflecting attacks in the course of your training, it will become ingrained and you will be inadvertently influenced by the enemy's ploys. The Way of combat strategy is direct and true, and it is vital to employ correct principles when assailing the enemy so that he is the one who succumbs to you. Study this well.

(4) About Schools With Many Techniques
(一、他流に太刀数多き事)

Teaching myriad sword techniques is essentially exploiting the Way as a commercial venture. By bamboozling novices with countless moves, teachers make them believe that their training method is profound. This approach in strategy should be rejected. Thinking there are assorted ways to strike a man with a sword is indicative of a confused mind. There are not so many ways to cut in the world. Irrespective of whether the swordsman is a master, a novice, a woman or a child, approaches for striking or cutting are limited. The only other techniques [apart from cutting] are to stab or slash. There cannot be multiple variations if the point is simply to cut.

Nevertheless, depending on the place and according to the conditions, you will be unable to wield your sword if stuck in a position that is restricted above and to the sides. This is why I have five ways for holding the sword [so that any situation can be dealt with rationally]. It does not comply with the true

Way to cut by twisting the wrists, swiveling the body, leaping or circling. A twisting cut, swiveling cut, leaping cut or skirting cut will never cut. These movements are totally ineffectual.

In my strategy, the body and mind are kept straight while the opponent is made to twist and bend. It is important to defeat him just as his mind becomes distorted. Be sure to research this well.

(5) Schools That Emphasize Sword Stances
（一、他流に太刀の構を用る事）

It is a mistake attaching too much importance to sword stances. That there are [so many] stances [emphasized] in the world of sword strategy implies that there are no enemies to fight.[7] To be more explicit, inventing new laws from old customs to suit current rules should not happen in the Way of combat strategy. Simply coerce the enemy into a compromised position as each situation allows. Assuming a fighting stance means adopting a posture that is immovable and resolute [both in body and mind]. Like building a castle or positioning one's troops, be prepared to withstand any assault with an impenetrable mind. This is fundamental. In the Way of combat strategy, one must strive to take the initiative at all times. To [carelessly] assume a stance is a declaration of your intention to wait for the opponent to move. Consider this with caution. In the Way of combat strategy, it is mandatory to unsettle the enemy's stance, assail him in ways he least expects, make him panic, irritate him, intimidate him and triumph by capitalizing on his confused cadence. I am thus averse to stances if it means

---

[7] It had been almost a decade since the last major military campaign (Shimabara Rebellion). At the time Musashi wrote his treatise, Japan was enjoying a period of peace.

relinquishing the initiative. That is why I teach the *ukō-mukō* or "stance [of] no-stance" in my school.

In large-scale strategy, you must know the numbers and strength of the enemy, take into consideration the lay of the battlefield and be aware of your own numbers and ability. It is essential in war to position your troops in the most favorable site before the battle begins. It is twice as advantageous to take the initiative and attack first rather than wait for the enemy to do so. Assuming an unflinching sword stance to parry an attack is effectively the same as constructing a [protective] fence of pikes and glaives. When you strike the enemy, pull the "fence posts" out and use them as pikes and glaives. Study this carefully.

(6) About "Fixing the Gaze" in Other Schools
(一、他流に目付と云事)

Certain schools maintain that the gaze should be fixed on the enemy's sword. Others teach students to focus on the hands, the face, the enemy's feet and so on. Setting your gaze on specific points will cause uncertainty and will adversely affect your strategy. To give another example, players of *kemari*[8] do not focus intently on the ball as they kick it. They can still deflect the ball off their temple and kick it using the *bansuri* technique[9] or keep it afloat with an *oimari* kick,[10] or even a spin kick. As the player becomes more accomplished, he can kick

---

[8] *Kemari* is a traditional game in which the players (usually eight) form a circle and kick a deerskin ball 9.4 inches (24 cm) in diameter among each other without letting it fall to the ground. Players can use any part of their body except their arms and hands to keep the ball in the air. *Kemari* became a popular pastime among court nobles from the eighth century but later spread to warriors and commoners.

[9] Volley off the back of the foot.

[10] Perhaps similar to the "neck-stall" trick in freestyle soccer.

the ball without needing to look at it. The same can be said of acrobats. Someone accustomed to this art can juggle several swords while simultaneously balancing a door on the tip of his nose. He has no need to fix his gaze as he can see what he is doing intuitively through lots of training. Likewise, in the Way of combat strategy, the warrior learns through engaging with different opponents to determine the weight of an enemy's mind. With practice in the Way, you will come to see everything, from reach to the speed of the sword. Generally speaking, "fixing the gaze" in strategy is to attach it to an enemy's mind.

In large-scale strategy, also, the state and numbers of the enemy must be scrutinized. The two approaches for observing are the eyes of *kan* ("looking in") and *ken* ("looking at"). Intensifying the *kan* gaze, penetrate the enemy's mind to discern the conditions. With a widened gaze, examine how the battle is progressing and search for moments of strength and vulnerability. This is the surest way to victory. In both large- and small-scale strategy, refrain from fixing your gaze narrowly. As I have written previously, focusing on minute details will make you forget bigger issues. Your mind will become confused and certain victory will slip from your reach. You must study this principle through careful training.

(7) About Footwork in Other Schools
(一、他流に足づかひ有事)

There are several types of footwork employed in other schools, such as "floating foot,"[11] "jumping foot," "hopping foot," "trampling foot" and "crow's foot."[12] These are all deficient from the

---

[11] The body weight is centered on the back foot and the front foot is raised above the ground.

[12] Hopping like a bird in a diagonal direction.

perspective of my school of strategy. The reason why "floating foot" is to be avoided is because your feet will try to hover in combat when you should, in fact, always move with your feet firmly planted on the ground. "Jumping foot" should also be avoided because there is always a preparatory movement at the start and a sense of finality when you land. "Jumping foot" is worthless as there is no need to leap around continually in battle. "hopping foot" causes the mind to "bounce" as well as the feet and you will be unable to advance. "Stomping foot" is particularly unacceptable as the feet are planted with an attitude of waiting. Then there are the supple methods for maneuvering, such as "crow's foot." Sword fights take place in all kinds of environment: swamps, boggy ground, mountains, rivers, stony fields or narrow pathways. Depending on the location, it may be impractical to leap around or move nimbly.

In our school, nothing about the feet changes. It is no different from routinely walking down a road. In accordance with the enemy's cadence, when hurrying, do so with an unhurried bearing without moving too little or too much, ensuring that your steps do not become inconsistent.

Movement is also critical in large-scale strategy. If you attack the enemy hastily without judging their intentions, your cadence will become chaotic and it will be difficult to succeed. Conversely, delaying too much will lead to missing the chance to strike and finish the encounter quickly as your enemy falters and starts to crumble. Strike the instant you detect disarray, not giving the enemy any mercy or chances to regroup. This is how victory is attained. Train hard in this.

(8) The Use of Speed in Other Schools
(一、他の兵法にはやきを用る事)

Speed in combat is irrelevant in the real Way. In all things, what is referred to as "fast" means that the intervals are out of sync with the rhythm. This is what is meant when things are said to be fast or slow. The movements of a master in some discipline will not appear to be fast. For example, there are messengers capable of covering 40–50 leagues [120–150 miles] in a day but they are not running at full pace from morning to night. Tenderfoot runners will never cover such a long distance even if they run all day. In the Way of dance,[13] a novice accompanying a skilled singer in the recital of a song will become harried as he struggles not to fall behind. In the same way, a novice playing the drum in the placid melody of the "Oimatsu" play[14] will feel like he is lagging and will try to catch up in a hurry. The tempo for "Takasago"[15] is faster, but it is incorrect to play it hastily. He who hurries falls down and will end up being too slow. Slowness is also not good. Those who are highly accomplished may seem slow but they never lose their timing. Whatever the case, a skilled practitioner never appears to be rushed.

These examples should help you to understand the principles of the Way. Going too fast is particularly bad in the Way of combat. Depending on the location, be it marshland, swampy terrain or the like, it may be impossible to maneuver the body and legs speedily. With the sword as well, do not cut too quickly. Not being like a [*tessen* iron] fan[16] or a knife, if you

---

[13] Noh theater.

[14] "Aged Pine," attributed to Zeami Motokiyo (1363–1443).

[15] "High Sand" is a play by Zeami set in the region where Musashi was born. A Shinto priest travels to Takasago, a pine-forested beach in Harima province, where he meets an aged couple sweeping the forest floor. They tell him that two ancient pine trees, one there at Takasago and the other at Sumiyoshi in Settsu province, are husband and wife, and although they are separated by a great distance, their hearts are one. The couple reveal they are the spirits of the two trees and then disappear.

[16] An iron war fan (*tessen*). An expert in *tessen-jutsu* used solid or folding

try to cut quickly with a sword, the speed will prevent it from cutting. Consider this point carefully.

In the case of large-scale strategy as well, the thought of rushing things is hazardous. So long as you employ the mindset of "stopping the start," then you will never be too slow. You must take the opposite approach in situations when somebody is moving with great speed. It is important to keep calm without being unduly influenced [by your opponent]. Be sure to train hard and work out the meaning of this.

(9) About "Interior" and "Exterior" Teachings in Other Schools (一、他流に奥表と云事)

In combat, what are "exterior" and "interior" teachings? Depending on the art, terms such as "ultimate teaching" are used along with "interior" or "exterior." As for the principles of combatting an enemy with a sword, there is no such thing as fighting with exterior techniques and cutting with interior teachings.

In teaching my method of combat, those new to the Way are first taught techniques that are easy to do and principles that are easy to grasp. Later, I impart deeper, more diverse principles that students can pick up naturally as they progress down the path. Whatever the case, experience [of actual combat] is the only way to remember the teachings, so there is no distinction between "interior" and "exterior."

As it is said, "Venturing into the depths of the mountain, deciding to go even further in, one will emerge once again at an entrance." Regardless of the Way, sometimes the "interior" is better and sometimes it is better to show the exterior. With

---

iron fans, usually with eight to ten wood or iron ribs, to fight adversaries wielding swords or spears. *Tessen* could also be used for fending off knives and projectile weapons, and could be thrown itself.

the principles of combat, who can say what should be hidden and what should be revealed? This is why I dislike asking students to submit written pledges of secrecy under the threat of punishment when I teach them my Way. Instead, I gauge the students' capability and teach the correct Way, encouraging them to discard bad habits from the five or six realms of strategy.[17] The student is taught how to enter into the true path of warrior principles and to liberate his mind from the shackles of doubt. This is the Way of teaching in my school. This requires considerable training.

Hitherto in the Wind Scroll, I recorded in concise terms the strategy of other schools in nine articles. I could follow with more detailed accounts exposing gateways to interior teachings of each of these schools. I have refrained, however, from naming schools and their technical labels as explanations for such and such a way varies from person to person and their interpretation of the principles. As such, even within the same school, adherents will have a slightly different interpretation of their methods. I did not identify the schools or techniques because they are sure to change with time.

I have summarized the conventional traits of various schools in these nine points. From a broad perspective and from the standpoint of proper reasoning, clearly these schools are biased with their preference for either longer weapons, or by asserting the advantages of short swords, or their obsession with strength and weakness, coarseness and refinement.

---

[17] Musashi uses the term *godo-rokudo* here, alluding to the Five or Six Realms of Existence in Buddhist thought as an analogy to explain harmful or misguided habits picked up in the study of strategy (Uozumi, Ibid., p. 168). The (Five) Six Realms are a description of conditioned existence into which beings are reborn. They include the Hell Realm, the Realm of Hungry Ghosts, the Animal Realm, [the Realm of Asura (Titans)], the Human Realm and the Realm of Devas (Gods) and Heavenly Beings.

As these schools all represent biased Ways, there is no need to explicitly state the "gateway" or "inner sanctions" as everybody knows what they are. In my school, there is no such thing as "interior" or "gateway" for sword work.[18] There are no set fighting stances per se. It is simply to learn the virtues with all one's heart. This is of the essence in strategy.

12th Day of the 5th Month, Shōhō 2 (1645)
Shinmen Musashi Genshin
[To] Terao Magonojō

---

[18] The term Musashi uses for exterior is *omote* and interior is *oku*. *Omote* techniques are the representative surface or "gateway" techniques and the first ones a novice will learn in a martial art school. Contrasted to this are the *ura* or *oku* "interior" teachings. These are essentially the secret most teachings of a school and are only taught to advanced students. Musashi also employs these terms in Niten Ichi-ryū, but unlike his contemporaries he attaches no particular arcane meaning to them. His mantra was simply to learn the fundamentals thoroughly without concern for any esoteric nonsense. By painstakingly researching the basics for years in the cauldron of combat, eventually the swordsman would arrive at a profound understanding of his Way as long as he kept to the true path. Over philosophizing of this ideal was a detour from the true path of swordsmanship, and that is what Musashi is indicating here.

The Ether Scroll

Kū-no-Maki

空 の 巻

Main Points

* *Otherwise known as Void, Emptiness, Nothingness or Heaven, here Musashi explains the true meaning of Ether.*

* *He explains that Ether is not related to the Buddhist concept of Nirvana or enlightenment, but it is an enlightened state of sorts in that everything becomes crystal clear.*

* *Breaking through, breaking free, freedom in all Ways is the essence of Ether.*

* *This final Scroll in Gorin-no-sho was probably not completed by Musashi before he handed the manuscript to his student one week before his death.*

* *Translation source is Uozumi Takashi's Teihon Gorin-no-sho, pp. 170-72.*

Introduction

The Way of combat in Nitō Ichi-ryū is made clear in the Ether Scroll.[1] The Ether is a place where there is nothing. I consider this emptiness as something which cannot be known. Of course, Ether is also nothing. Knowing what does exist, one can then know what does not. This is what I mean by "Ether." People tend to mistake this notion of Ether as something that cannot be distinguished but this is not the true Ether. It is simply confusion in everybody's minds. So too in the Way of combat strategy, ignorance of the laws of the samurai by those who practice the Way of the warrior is not represented as emptiness. Likewise, those who harbor various doubts explain it as "emptiness," but this is not the true meaning of Ether.

The warrior must scrupulously learn by heart the Way of combat strategy and thoroughly study other martial arts without forgoing any aspect related to the practice of the warrior's Way. He must seek to put the Way into practice each hour of every day without tiring or losing focus. He must polish the two layers of his mind, the "heart of perception" and the "heart of intent," and sharpen his two powers of observation, the gazes of *kan* ("looking in") and *ken* ("looking at"). He must recognize that the true Ether is where all the clouds of confusion have completely lifted, leaving not a hint of haziness.

---

[1] I use the term "Ether" knowing that there may be some objection. The word "ether" as used in English has its roots in late fourteenth-century French and means "upper regions of space." This is taken directly from the Latin term *aether* ("the upper pure, bright air"). In ancient cosmology, ether was considered a purer form of fire or air, or as a fifth element. This understanding of the term seems to fit extremely well with the Japanese term *kū*, which is usually translated as "void." Of course, this is not wrong, nor are other translations, such as "emptiness." "Ether" just seems to strike the right cord with me in terms of etymology and philosophy. Confusion can arise when Musashi uses the term *kū* in different contexts. In such cases, I use other translations, such as "void" and "empty," but the actual title of the scroll and the concept Musashi is espousing, I translate as "Ether."

When you are impervious to the true Way, faithfully following your own instead thinking all is well, be it Buddhist Law or secular law, you will stray further from the truth. When the spirit is uncurled and compared with overarching universal principles, it becomes evident that a prejudiced mind and a distorted view of things have led to a departure from the proper path. Know this mind and use what is straight as your foundation. Make the sincere heart your Way as you practice strategy in its broadest sense, correctly and lucidly. Ponder the Ether as you study the Way. As you practice the Way, the Ether will open before you.

There is Good, not Evil in the Ether
There is Wisdom
There is Reason
There is the Way
The Mind, Empty

12th Day of the 5th Month, Shōhō 2 (1645)
Shinmen Musashi Genshin
[To] Terao Magonojō

Memorial of Musashi's duels with Yoshioka swordsmen in Ichijoji Sagarimatsu-cho, Kyoto. (Shinsendo Temple)

MIRROR ON THE WAY OF COMBAT

HEIDŌKYŌ

兵 道 鏡

Main Points

* Musashi created his Enmei-ryū school in 1604 after defeating the celebrated Yoshioka swordsmen in a series of duels, and wrote this treatise the following year.

* The title Heidōkyō indicates that Musashi considered his comprehension of the Way of combat to be lucid and clear, like a polished mirror.

* Heidōkyō was written as a catalogue of techniques and teachings to present to excellent disciples in recognition of their mastery of the Enmei-ryū. The first recipient of this document was Ochiai Chūe'mon.

* Although the first document consisted of twenty-eight articles, sometime later Musashi rewrote some of the articles and added new sections outlining more techniques and procedures, making thirty-six articles in all.

* *The content is practical and surprisingly open, albeit a challenge for the uninitiated to follow in many places. Although the techniques are difficult to decipher and would have required supplementary technical and verbal instruction (as Musashi often states in the text), Heidōkyō can be considered one of the earliest known expositions of the technical curriculum of any martial art school in Japan. For this reason, it is quite revolutionary.*

* *Not surprisingly, at this early stage of Musashi's brilliant career there is considerable overlap with some of the teachings in his adoptive father's school, Tōri-ryū, but Heidōkyō is testament to his ability and combat experience.*

* *There are variants of Heidōkyō and it was unclear whether Musashi actually wrote the text. Professor Uozumi Takashi was able to corroborate that it was in fact written by Musashi. This translation source and comparative observations are from Uozumi Takashi,* Miyamoto Musashi: Nihonjin no Michi, *pp. 264–93. Reference is also made to possible reconstructions of the techniques in Akabane Tatsuo's recent book* Musashi Muhai no Gihō.

◎ Similar articles in *Gorin-no-sho* and *Heihō Sanjūgo-kajō*

○ Similar article in *Gorin-no-sho*

● Similar article in *Heihō Sanjūgo-kajō*

△ Later addition in *Heidōkyō* 36

---

(1) The Mindset of Strategy and Positioning
(心持ちの事　付　座之次第) ◎

With regards to mindset as you engage in a contest, be calmer than normal and try to see into your opponent's mind. The enemy whose voice becomes higher in pitch, eyes widen, face reddens, muscles bulge and face grimaces is basically incompetent and will [clumsily] hit through to the ground. When faced with a [second-rate] adversary such as this, maintain serenity of mind and observe his face dispassionately so as not to provoke him. Then, taking hold of your sword, smile and assume a position lower than the upper stance (*jōdan*). Coolly evade his blow as he tries to attack you. When the enemy appears somewhat perturbed by your unusual attitude, this is the time to strike.

Also, if your opponent is quiet, eyes narrowed, body at ease, and he is holding his sword in a relaxed manner as if his fingers are floating on the hilt, assume that he is an expert. Do not saunter carelessly into his range. You must seize the initiative and assail him skillfully, driving him back and striking in quick succession. If you are nonchalant with such a competent opponent, he will force you back. It is crucial to ascertain how capable your enemy is.

In terms of where you should position yourself, the same conditions apply in both spacious or cramped locations. Step in so that walls will not impede your sword swings from either side. Take an approximate stance with the long sword and nimbly close in on your foe. If your sword should collide with some barrier, the enemy will become emboldened and will hem you in. If your sword looks as if it might scrape the ceiling, determine the actual height with the tip and be mindful thereafter. You can employ either sword for this, as long as it is the one that cannot be used [in attack while you do this]. Keep the light behind you. With your usual training, be prepared to freely apply any kind of technique with a relaxed mind, but always execute with urgency. It is important to adapt according to the circumstances.

(2) About Gaze （目付之事）◎

Direct your eyes on the enemy's face. Do not focus on anything else. Since the mind is projected in [facial] expressions, there is no place more revealing than the face to fix one's gaze. The way of observing the enemy's face is the same as looking through the mist at trees and rocks on an island two and a half miles [4 km] in the distance. It is the same as peering at [and identifying] birds perched atop a shanty 100 yards [91 meters] away through the falling sleet. It is also akin to beholding a decorative wooden board used to cover the ridge and purlin ends of a roof gable or the tiles on a hut. Calmly focus your gaze [to take everything in]. It is a mistake to look at the place you intend to strike. Do not move your head to the side. Feign inattentiveness as you observe the enemy's entire body at once. Furrow your brows as you peer but do not wrinkle your forehead. This cannot be conveyed with words and letters.[1]

(3) Taking Hold of the Sword （太刀取り様之事）◎

In taking hold of the sword(s), your index fingers and thumbs should float with your other fingers and your thumbs grasping firmly. The same principles apply to the way the hilt is held for both the right and left hands. Swords are brought together with the tip of the short sword at a position six inches [15 cm] over and approximately seven inches [18 cm] forward of the long sword's guard (*tsuba*). It is not good to see when the elbow(s) bent [in the cut], to have the arm(s) too rigid as this will impede movement. It is best to angle your right elbow about three inches [7 cm] and your left elbow around

---

[1] Musashi uses the Buddhist term *Kyōgai-betsuden* here and in other places which I have translated as such. In the Buddhist context, it literally means "revelation through intuitive discernment."

four inches [10 cm]. It is also not good to see when the wrists are bent or extended. Be sure to remove the tautness in your muscles. Taking your long sword in the correct manner means you are able to strike the enemy spontaneously. This is why this instruction is fundamental. There are oral teachings.

4) About Closing the Distance When Facing Off
(太刀合いを積る之事) ●

When closing in on your opponent, the position six inches [15 cm] from the sword tip is the "past" (*kako*), the "percussion point" (*monouchi*)[2] of the blade is the "present" (*genzai*), and the point of contact is the "future" (*mirai*).[3] After unsheathing your long sword,[4] take the initiative from the "past" position and advance by sliding your tip through to the opponent's "present" and strike immediately. Entering from "past" to "present" is achieved by using your sword to "ride" over the top, or detach from or evade [the enemy's sword]. Do not to falter when you reach the "present." You are likely to miss if you strike from the "past." If you strike too deeply from the "present," then you will end up "hitting the ground." Any closer, however, and you should grab hold of him. Stopping at this point is dangerous as well. It is vital to cover the distance with your whole body. To be conveyed orally.

---

[2] Location of the "percussion point" (*monouchi*) of a sword depends entirely on its overall length. For example, in the case of a sword measuring 2 feet 4.7 inches (72.8 cm), the percussion point would be located around 6–11 inches (15–30 cm) from the tip. The percussion point is the "sweet spot" of the blade which is used for cutting.

[3] Musashi appropriated these terms from his father's Tōri-ryū.

[4] Musashi taught that if there was time, the short sword should be drawn first and transferred to the left hand, and then the long sword should be unsheathed after this. If the enemy is already moving in, the long sword should be drawn first and the short sword only when the opportunity arises.

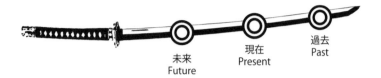

未来
Future

現在
Present

過去
Past

(5) About Footwork (足遣い之事) ◎

In terms of how to use your feet, move in without hesitation the moment you draw your sword. When you ride through to the enemy's "present," strike with your feet in unison [with the sword]. After drawing your long sword, move around and in from the right if it is difficult to attack. If you move around to the left, you will be too far away, leaving you with little room to maneuver. Seeing your stance with the long sword at the ready, if the enemy moves to the left, follow and then move back again. Immediately take the initiative to drive him back and capitalize on his surprise. As he is startled, you will clearly see the place to strike him[as he reacts]. Never drop your guard here. Strike keenly without moving in [too] deeply. It is important to adapt according to the circumstances.

(6) About Posture (身之懸之事) ◎

Regarding posture, lower your face slightly without making a [tense] "bull neck" and open your shoulders. Do not stick out your chest but thrust out your stomach. Keep your backside in and your hips steady. Bend your knees slightly and tread firmly with your heels. Your toes should be light and pointing outward. When you strike, keep your face the same [down-ward angle], contract your neck [like a bull], stick out your chest and backside, straighten your knees, lift your heels up and stand strongly on your toes. Strike while lifting your left foot up. Do not relinquish your guard after the strike. Glare at your opponent. The moment he lifts his head up, strike him down emphatically. Conveyed orally.

Omote Procedures
(Seven Dual-Sword Forms)

△ (36-7) About "Maehachi-no-Kurai (Chūdan)" (前ハ之位之事)

(7) About "Extended Cut" (指合ぎりの事)

In *sashiai-giri* (extended cut), point your long sword at the enemy's right eye at the "past" position. As he strikes, pull your shoulder away and evade the blow [by lifting the hands overhead] completely without bending your elbows and wrists. Step forward with the right foot as the long sword is raised overhead, and move your left foot up in quick succession, followed by a big step with the right again as the enemy retreats. [While moving forward] The long sword is down and [pointing to the] back on to the left knee [and with the short sword pointing at his face]: [as the enemy attacks again] block the blow by cutting up just below the "percussion point" (*monouchi*) [on your long sword] near his sword guard. Step in and place your left foot below his groin as you wedge the [crossed] swords into his neck [forcing him down]. The enemy will try to somehow get on top of you. He may also try to seize your sword. Smash down on his chest with your left foot. It is important to adapt according to the circumstances.

(8) About Detaching from "Change" (転変はづす位之事)

In *tenpen-no-kurai* (change), the stance is the same as that for *sashiai-giri* [no. 7]. Join your two swords in the "past" positions (*mawari-no-tōri*).[5] As the enemy cuts down [at your crossed swords], dodge the blow and then cross again atop of his "present" [to wedge his sword down] and move in. As he moves away, open [your swords] to release and follow with both of your swords extended and crossed at the front [with the tips pointing at the enemy]. As he once again attempts to cut down on your swords with all of his strength, open your swords and move the long sword away. Then [as the enemy lifts his sword overhead again] keep your short sword (left hand) in front and pointing at his face while bringing your long sword vigorously back over your left shoulder. Then step in with the right foot and lift your left foot high to the front as you cut and the enemy horizontally across his upper arm [with your long sword] as he pulls up [after attempting to cut you left hand?]. To be conveyed orally.

(9) Same as above (Change) "Striking Down"
(同、打落さるゝ位)

The stance and entry [to suppress the enemy's sword] for the *uchi-otosaruru* (striking down) procedure is the same as [8] above. Your feet are together when taking the guard position. Step out with the right foot to ride over the opponent's sword in the crossed (*mawari-no-tōri*) position. With swords extended, the opponent will attempt to strike them out of your hand with force. Drop your swords down naturally [to avoid the strike]. Keeping your head perfectly still, extend your short sword (left hand) and assume a stance to the front left. When the enemy attempts to cut at your [extended left] hand, pull it back over your right shoulder while cutting up at the enemy's arms from

---

[5] Similar in form to the *chūdan* position on page 89, but with the swords actually crossed in front.

below with your long sword as if to parry the blow. You must be relaxed. It is important to adapt according to the circumstances.

(10) About "In-no-Kurai (Yin)" and "Katsu-Totsu"
(陰位之事 付 喝吐)

With *in-no-kurai*,[6] face the front then step forward with your left foot slightly and your left arm extended so that the tip of your short sword is pointing at the opponent's left eye. Take your long sword vertically up into the *jōdan* position [to your right side]. With distance closed in the front [so that the tip of your short sword comes into contact with the enemy's], cut passed your short sword onto the enemy's hands.

With *katsu-totsu* (cut-thrust, thrust-cut), [with both swords in the lowered position] move your left foot forward while directing the tip of your long sword at the enemy, revealing to him the back edge (*mine*) of the blade. When the enemy attacks [and tries to hot your sword out of the way], thrust your [right] arm out and cut quickly from the tip [by using the momentum generated in deflecting the enemy's blow to whip your long sword around to the neck]. The faster and harder the strike is, the better. Step forward with your right foot as you strike. If the distance is too great to follow through with *katsu-kotsu*, pull your [back] foot up [to close the gap]. If the distance is suitable, switch your feet on the spot as you attack. If you are close, pull your right foot back as you execute *katsu-totsu* in the same position. When using a shorter long sword, deflect (*uke-nagashi*) the enemy's blow and then strike. *Katsu-totsu* is ineffective when the distance is too close. In such a situation, be prepared to thrust the enemy in the chest. It is important to adapt according to the circumstances.

---

6 Also pronounced as *kage-no-kurai*.

(11) About "Yō-no-Kurai (Yang)" and Mindset for "Evasion" (陽位之事　付たり　貫く心持ち) ○

With *yō-no-kurai*, shift your short sword in accordance with the enemy's stance and make a cross [in relation to the enemy's sword] while extending your right arm to assume the left-side stance (*hidari-wakigamae*) [with the long sword pointing back on the left side of the body]. [As the enemy cuts down from the overhead stance] cut up at his hands from below with the long sword. It is better if the long sword cuts to the upper *jōdan* stance. Edge forward from your right foot with your hand directed to the right as you hit.

The mindset for evasion[7] (*nuku*) is to employ the same cadence as the enemy as he cuts down to smash your long sword as your strike up from below. Show that you are going to clash [with equal force], then [deflect rather than block his blade] swing your long sword around [using the momentum to follow through] and cut his neck [on his left side]. If the enemy does not attack with force, then there is no need to employ this method. It is important to cross your hands[8] and cut his hands [from below with the long sword]. To be conveyed orally.

(12) Same as above (Yang) "Slap and Advance" (同位　はる積之事)

With *haru-tsumori* (slap and advance), enter to the "present" point with the tip of your long sword, extend your arms and place the long sword to your left side [with the tip pointing back] as you pivot the right side of your body forward. Then turn your [right] hand in and slap diagonally upward from below in a relaxed fashion. When the enemy attacks with force

---

[7]　A variation of the same technique.

[8]　Left hand on top and right hand on the bottom.

parry the blow powerfully with your long sword keep the same footwork, body movement and cadence, and reveal your intention to meet force with force with your long sword. As the enemy applies more force to his strike from above, deflect [and use the generated momentum to swing your sword around] and cut [his neck]. It is not effective if you are too close. Again, if he attacks quickly, thrust from underneath as if to deflect, but extend out to strike his hands. Many oral teachings.

(13) About "Jōkatō" (定可当之事)

In *jōkatō*, the left foot and side of the body are slightly forward with the point of your short sword and the enemy's long sword meeting at the "past" point. This is your fixed position to strike (*jōkatō*). [For the stance] Push the tip of your long sword forward [crossing in front of your body with the short sword] with your chest open to make your body look large. As if hugging a big tree, curve your elbows but do not bend your wrists. [As the enemy cuts down at the two crossed swords] step forward with the left foot while turning your right hand to cut up through the enemy's hands, then step forward with the right foot as you flip the long sword back down quickly to cut the enemy's neck. Stretch out your right arm with the upward cut. Lift your right foot as you parry up and stamp the ground as you deliver the downward blow. It is important to adapt.

Kachimi-no-Kurai
(Seven Dual-Sword Methods for Winning)

(14) About Taking the Initiative (先を懸くる位之事) ◎

There are various ways to initiate an attack. If the enemy is holding his sword in the middle *chūdan* or lower *gedan* position, assume the *in-no-kurai* stance[9] make noise with your feet as you immediately assail the enemy showing a strong resolve to strike, waving your long sword slightly as you charge into the "past" point. By moving in briskly and forcing the enemy back, he will absolutely retaliate. If he retreats, close in further. If the enemy is ready in the upper *jōdan* position, assume the lower *gedan* position and move in from your left foot, projecting that you are about to rush him. If you show you will cut at his neck, he will panic and retaliate Here, you would normally assume the *sashiai-giri* position [no. 7 above]. When you reach the "past" point, lift up on your back foot and prepare to strike down by raising your long sword 12 inches [30 cm], aiming at his neck to drive him back. You can take the initiative with either sword. Do not do what he expects. Catch him off guard by changing rhythm and take the initiative. Do not engage if you sense he knows what you are going to do. Oral instruction.

(15) About "Kissaki-gaeshi" (切先返し之事) ◎

To execute *kissaki-gaeshi* [swinging the sword(s) alternately cutting up and down], the tip of your long sword rides up to the "present." As you bring your feet together, aim for the mark as you change the sword to the opposite trajectory. If your target is clear and your opponent is close, turn the blade instantly with a small motion. If you are a little far away, prepare to turn your hands quickly as you exhale and enter forcefully with your body and legs aiming to cut his hands on the downward cut. When the enemy attacks you, pull your hand back to the right to evade while simultaneously preparing to counter. Throw your long sword out to cut in a large motion [while

---

9 The left hand holding the short sword at the opponent's face and the long sword held vertically in the right hand at the side of the head.

blocking with the short sword] as you take a big step forward with the right foot to trap his left leg as you strike at his neck. The blade is then swung around to cut vertically through his nasal bridge. Coming off the strike, step back and adopt the *yō-no-kurai* position (*hidari wakigamae*) [no. 11]. The feeling to slash is the same as before. This cannot be conveyed with words and letters.

(16) About Striking the Legs (足を打つ位之事)

There are three ways to strike your opponent's legs. If he is in the *gedan* position to the right rear, hold your long sword slightly higher than *gedan* and move it around as if to bring it to your left shoulder. When your long sword's tip reaches the "present" point, do not stop but keep moving your feet quickly as you enter deeply, then strike him as he steps back. Never look down at your feet or give away your intended target as you strike as swiftly as you can with *kissaki-gaeshi*. If in close, receive his attack [with the short sword] as you cut. If the enemy is holding his sword in a high position, also assume the *jōdan* higher stance [with the long sword], look up and move in quickly to the "present" position to strike at his legs. Immediately go back into *yō-no-kurai* irrespective if you hit or not [to execute *kissaki-gaeshi* as he strikes from above]. Also, when the enemy tries to attack from above the middle stance, turn the blade of your long sword and bend your elbow to bring it to your right side ready for *kissaki-gaeshi*, but then strike down at his legs. As he blocks from above, cut at the legs again as you go back to assume half-*jōdan* but always ready to execute *kissaki-gaeshi*. It is important to adapt according to the circumstances.

(17) About Attacking the Arms (手を打つ位の事)

When the enemy has assumed a stance with his sword extended to the front in a position lower than *chūdan* to the right, lower the tip of your long sword and advance from "past" to the "present." From there deliver a punchy strike to his hands. When the cut goes through it should go no more than 12 inches [30 cm] before cutting down on [with *kissaki-gaeshi*] from the apex, and must be vigorous and fast. The smaller and stronger the strike, the better. If his blade is to the left, lower your hands, cross your two swords and attach them to the enemy's. Slash at the fingernails on the enemy's right hand by directly moving the long sword up 12 inches [30 cm]. If the enemy is fast, do a traversing crosscut. It is important to maneuver quickly and not leave yourself open. Oral teaching.

△ (36-19) The Mindset for Thrusting (春く心持の事)

(18) About "Disengaging the Sword Tip" (切先外す位の事)

Disengaging the sword is done by moving the shoulders and hands. However, it is bad to move your hands too much. Disengaging to the left is done with a swift movement. When disengaging the right, lift up a little higher, then resume your stance. Step out with your right foot when disengaging with the left hand, and with your left foot when disengaging with the right hand. As soon as you have disengaged, strike at the enemy's arms without giving him a chance to attack. It is not good to spin to the side when cutting. Conveyed orally.

(19) About "Riding" (乗る位の事)

The approach of "riding" is not only sliding over [the enemy's sword] with your swords. Neither is it just riding with your arms, elbows, shoulders, hips or feet. It means that as soon as your opponent unleashes an attack, you must envelop him with your whole body at once, riding in from the sword tip to the tips of the toes. When the enemy moves his sword, ride up it without delay. When the "present" point is passed, keep following through and ride into him without stepping back even if your swords do not meet. Move slightly faster than a walking and mount the enemy without hesitation. When he blinks, stop suddenly and cut his hands. Further instructions conveyed orally.

(20) About "Shuffling Feet" (すり足の事)

"Shuffling feet" (*suriashi*) is used when the enemy is complacent and has both hands on his sword in the *chūdan* middle stance, or suchlike. As you draw your long sword, step out slightly with your left foot, bring your hands together lightly clasped, hips settled, and face your opponent front on. When he is about to attack, step out a little more with the left foot and then leap in suddenly with the right foot, bending at the left knee [to lower your body] as you counter the blow by cutting up [at the hands] from underneath. This must be executed with considerable power. Do not hesitate even a little. This cannot be conveyed with words and letters.

Oku (Interior)
Ura Maeroku (Reverse Set of Six Forms)

△ (36-23) Genken Shikigen (眼見色現)

△ (36-24) Jimon Shōshutsu (耳聞声出)

△ (36-25) Binyū Kōken (鼻入香顕)

△ (36-26) Zettō Mibun (舌当味分)

△ (36-27) Shinshi Sokugyō (心思触行)

△ (36-28) Igo Hōgaku (意悟法学)

(21) About "Shin-no-Kurai" (真位の事)

With *shin-no-kurai* (the sword of truth), when the enemy is using two swords you can cut from the "past-past" position. Step out with your left foot as you bend your right knee [to lower your body] and swing with *jōkatō* [from the right-side stance], swapping your feet as you gauge the distance. Assume *yō-no-kurai* [left-side yang stance] and move in again to deflect the enemy's sword [cutting down from above], or change to *katsu-totsu* as you step out with your left foot and repeat the cut-thrust movement. Make sure your blows are powerful and continuous. It is vital that you take the initiative. It is also important to keep an eye on the enemy's short sword, and to not miss a beat. When the sides are restricted, step out with the left foot and stretch out, executing *katsu-totsu* as you extend and strike as many times as possible. Numerous oral instructions.

(22) About the "Two Swords of Existence and Nonexistence" (有無二剣の事)

Umu-no-niken (two swords of existence and nonexistence) is employed by holding the short sword up higher with the tip directed at the enemy, and the long word resting [back] on your left knee. When the enemy advances, slash his hands from underneath with the long sword while cutting down from above with the short sword. If the enemy does not assume the high guard when retreating and tries to hit your lower [right] hand, strike him with the short sword. If he seems preoccupied with your short sword strike upward with your long sword at both his hands. Do not get too close. For the stance, step out with your left foot while keeping your right foot 8–9 inches [20–23 cm] to the side. When constrained by space, leave your left foot where it is and step out with the right using this momentum to cut. It is important to adapt according to the circumstances.

(23) About "Throwing the Sword" (手離剣、打ち様の事)

Place your forefinger on the back of the short sword when executing *shuriken* (throwing the sword).[10] Keep your wrists firm and your shoulders relaxed and throw the blade as if thrusting at the enemy's "star"[11] where your eyes are fixed. It is because you are throwing with the image of cutting that the sword flies true. If you are close, throw the sword gently with the tip slightly up. When the distance is increased, with the enemy 6 feet [2 meters] away, lift the tip of the sword up about 6 inches [15 cm] to throw. If you are 9 feet [3 meters] away, lift the tip up 12 inches [30 cm] and 18 inches [45 cm] for a distance of 12 feet [3.6 meters]. It is not a problem to throw with the tip higher than the "star." The opposite is true, and it must never be lower. The more power you use to throw [in this case], the further the tip will fall and miss its mark with

---

[10] The term Musashi uses is *shuriken* but the ideograms are different to what most people envisage as small projectile weapons such as the fabled Ninja "throwing stars." The former uses the ideograms 手離剣, literally meaning "releasing sword from the hand." The latter is 手裏剣, "blade concealed [in] the hand." In any case, Musashi was apparently skilled in the art of projectile weapons. It is even said that he once defeated a sickle-and-chain wielding opponent by throwing his short sword at him.

[11] Musashi uses the term *hoshi* (star) as reference to the target being aimed for. This has all manner of connotations, including point, bull's-eye, a "star point on a Go board (an intersection traditionally marked with a small dot on the board), or "the star that determines one's fate."

a thud.[12] Refrain from bracing yourself too much when you throw. Look up and stick out your chest while stepping out. The more weight you have riding on the back [foot], the better. Perform one or two practice swings as you shout *Ei-Ei!* Load your body [like a spring] as you take a deep breath and then release it, yelling *Totsu!* Do not throw while vocalizing *Ei!* Practice this diligently.

(24) About "Fighting Many Opponents"
(多敵の位の事) ○

When facing multiple opponents, face the front and step out slightly with your left foot. Make sure that you are able to see all your opponents at once. Charge swiftly at the one who seems the strongest and cut him down first. The stance you take should be with the short sword pointing back to the left and the long sword back to the right. With both hands back, extend your posture with your chest and feet pushing forward and the tips of each sword almost meeting at the back. When you know that the enemy is in range, step out with your right foot and thrust both the long and short swords toward the enemy's eyes with the long sword hand [right] swinging up and then back down. Then, stepping out with the left foot, return to your original stance. Expand your chest as much as possible when swinging the swords. You should be able to hit enemies to your left side convincingly. It is important to adapt depending on the circumstances. Do not swing the swords too excessively, but be sure to take the initiative. Many oral teachings.

---

[12] It may hit the enemy, but it will not cut or pierce him.

(25) About "Taking the Hand"[13] (実手取りの事)

To apprehend an enemy who is holed up, [somebody else?] go toward the main entrance and probe each side of the doorway with a *yari* (pike). Hold your two swords together in a middle-low stance, draping clothing over the scabbard of the short sword. Step forward with your left foot and assume your stance. When you enter the house, rest the *yari* on your left shoulder and poke at the enemy's face. The enemy will frantically try to swat it away, thereby losing his composure. Assume a higher *chūdan* (middle) stance with the sword and block his attempts while discarding the clothing [concealing the swords]. Take hold of the blade of your short sword and hold it together with the back of your long sword as you push him away. Thrust at the enemy's chest as you pull his *wakizashi* (short sword) out. Then drop the swords while grabbing the enemy's right hand with your left before he can do anything. Quickly taking hold of his wrist, insert your long sword under his right side, pressing down on his chest and arm to knock him flat while stepping on his wrist and the hilt of his sword. Tie him up without delay. Keep the *yari* pressed against his face until he is completely subdued. Oral teaching.

(26) Drawing Swords of Different Lengths and Compatible Stances (太刀・刀、抜き合い様の事 付、あい太刀、あわざる太刀の事) ○

With regard to drawing long and short swords, when the interval [between you and the enemy] is 3–6 feet [1–1.8 meters]

---

[13] This is a play on words by Musashi. *Jitte* is one of the weapons he specialized in, but its literal meaning is "実 actual 手 hand." Although the name of the procedure indicates it involves a tussle with the *jitte*, it is actually a method for arresting an enemy holed up inside a building by "taking hold of his hands."

strike directly with your short sword. When it is further away, first draw your short sword [with your right hand] and quickly transfer it to your left. Unsheathe the long sword as you would in *yō-no-kurai* (yang posture) [no.11]. If the enemy attacks first, do not bother with the long sword. Strike his hand [immediately with the short sword] to prevent him from drawing. If the enemy does not attack, draw both of your swords as you please. If you have a smaller-sized *wakizashi*, which is easy to unsheathe [just with the left hand], coolly take out your long sword first and assume the upper stance (*jōdan*) as this will make it difficult for the enemy to approach. Also, with swords drawn, the position of *jōkatō* is useful against *hidarisha* (left diagonal) and *jōdan*-blocking *kasumi* stances. *In-no-kurai* (yin) is functional against *gedan* with both hands extended, and *chūdan*. *Katsu-totsu* is suitable against one-handed *chūdan* and one-handed left *jōdan*. *Yō-no-kurai* (yang) is useful against opponents in two-handed *jōdan*. You must consider your enemy's *engarde* stance and implement appropriate tactics. As for unsuitable measures, *jōkatō* is no good against the *migisha* (right diagonal) stance and one-handed *jōdan*. *In-no-kurai* is ineffectual against left diagonal, right diagonal and single-handed *jōdan* and *gedan* stances. *Katsu-totsu* will not work well against left diagonal, high single-handed stances to the right and the one-handed *gedan*. *Yō-no-kurai* is not compatible with left diagonal right diagonal, one-handed *jōdan* and *gedan* stances. *Katsumi-no-kurai* techniques are adjusted to the way the enemy holds his sword. There are many occasions in which *kissaki-gaeshi* and the like are not viable. Oral teachings.

(27) About the "Ultimate One-Sword Strike"
(是極一刀の事)

Zegoku-ittō (ultimate one-sword strike) is employed at times when you only have one sword unsheathed. If your opponent is skilled and there are few openings to exploit to achieve victory, take your sword back to your side, allowing plenty of space. Step out with your right foot, swing your sword once or twice, then retreat as you come into contact. Leaving your left foot where it is, observe the openings that arise as your opponent counters [your initial probing]. Strike as hard as you can at the "past" position with the long sword and swiftly unsheathe your short sword to cut his hand as he attempts to block. The shorter the [short] sword, the better when in close [as you can unsheathe it directly with your left hand]. When you have no recourse [to do anything else], this will lead to victory which is why it is the ultimate technique.[14]

(28) About the "Direct Path" (直通の位の事) ◎

Jikitsū-no-kurai ("direct path") is the soul of combat.[15] All the teachings I have outlined above are like parts of the human body.[16] Nothing more is needed. They must never be neglected. Depending on the situation, there are times when some techniques will not be suitable, but nothing will work without them [in your repertoire]. For example, the eyes, ears, nose, tongue, hands and feet are what our bodies are comprised of. If one of these things is missing, then we are incomplete. The sword techniques that I have conveyed must all be committed to memory and used intuitively. Without the soul and spirit of the "direct path," they amount to random madness. In all the

---

[14] Articles 26 and 27 are in the opposite order in *Heidōkyō 36*. Note that the technique starts as a one sword attack but finishes with two swords.

[15] Musashi refers to *Jikitsū* (直通) in later writings as *Jikidō* (直道). The ideogram 通 means "pass through" as well as "path" or "road." They mean essentially the same thing.

[16] Mind, eyes, feet, hands, mouth (shouts), etc.

techniques, be sure to seize the initiative and take the attack to the enemy. This will enable you to identify target areas.

You must then determine what techniques or guards will be effective and what are not viable in a particular situation. Gauge how to close the distance, then commit with single-minded resolve to follow through to your mark (star) and attack without deviating. For example, even if you have to deflect the whole world, the flight of your sword must not diverge from its path. Purge yourself of fear. When you know the moment for that one [direct and decisive] strike of *jikitsū*, let the power surge through you to deliver the cut. It is no different when you enter the opponent's space to arrest him. Advance rapidly, thinking of nothing other than grabbing hold of him. The further in you get, the better. Without the mind of "direct path," your swords will be lifeless. Even this and discover what it means. Even retreat counts as a loss. When we speak of the "interior" (deepest principles), nothing is deeper than this.

When we talk of the gateway (fundamental principles), nothing is more fundamental than this. The great monk Kūkai[17] traveled deep into the mountain when planning to construct a monastery in the innermost reaches of Mount Kōya. Thinking it was still not far enough, he continued walking further, but eventually came across dwellings again. He said, "The further I entered, the closer I came to human habitation; I had looked too far in."[18] The interior is not the interior. The gate is not the gate. There are no special, secret interior teachings to look for if the great wisdom of combat strategy surges through your sinews and veins. Just make sure

---

[17] Also known as Kōbō Daishi (774–835), Kūkai was a Buddhist priest of the early Heian period (794–1185) and the founder of the Shingon sect of esoteric Buddhism in Japan.

[18] He realized that passing through the interior he had come out the other side to the gate.

that nobody to your front or back can ever get the better of you. This cannot be conveyed with words and letters.

Upon mastering the secret techniques of my teacher[19] in the 10th month of Keichō 9 (1604), I resolved to outline the above 6 [+] 7 [+] 7 [+] 8 articles (= 28) in this "clear mirror" text as a record of my awareness.[20] I shall call it *Heidōkyō*—Mirror on the Way of Combat—and it shall be bestowed on my disciples to convey sublime teachings, serving as a license of proficiency (*menkyo-kaiden*). This unparalleled combat strategy of past and present will continue in an unbroken line for generations to come. This is why I have documented the secret teachings of my school, and it is what makes it an incomparable book of secrets. Even if someone has in their possession a license by my hand, if he does not also have this scroll then he is forbidden from employing the techniques and procedures of my school [in matches].[21] How can one possibly be victorious in a contest without absorbing these 28 articles? In light of an exemplary attitude [Ochiai Chūe'mon] to not share knowledge of the Enmei-ryū even with those closest, and dedication shown in the study of this school, I hereby confer this scroll authenticating attainment of the highest level of technical mastery in the Enmei-ryū. These are indeed the secret teachings.

Enmei-ryū "Champion of the Realm"
Miyamoto Musashi-no-Kami Fujiwara Yoshitsune
Auspicious Day, 12th Month, Keichō 10 (1605)

---

[19] Musashi's adoptive father, Munisai.

[20] "Clear mirror" in that the content is an "unclouded expose" of the combat methodology and philosophy of Musashi's Enmei-ryū school. This proclamation comes just after his famous victory over the Yoshioka clan in Kyoto.

[21] Musashi means that the swordsman cannot announce himself as a disciple of the Enmei-ryū when engaging in contests with adherents of other schools.

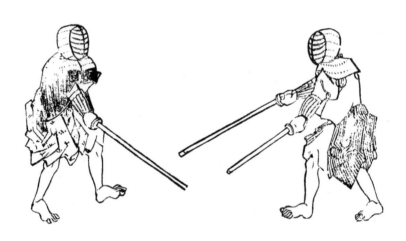

NOTES ON COMBAT STRATEGY

HEIHŌ-KAKITSUKE

兵 法 書 付

Main Points

* *Musashi did not personally name this document. Professor Uozumi Takashi called it* Heihō-kakitsuke *based on its content.*

* *It was written by Musashi in 1638 as a technical guide and transmission license for his students.*

* *Much of the content is further developed in* Heihō Sanjūgo-kajō, Heihō 39 *and* Gorin-no-sho *(Scrolls above).*

* *The section on the "Five Sword Stances" is very similar to what Terao Kumenosuke added to* Heihō Sanjūgo-kajō *in 1666. Kumenosuke arguably miswrote the terms and stances when he added articles to* Heihō 35 *to make* Heihō 39, *so the recent discovery of* Heihō-kakitsuke *has disentangled many points of confusion.*

* *Heihō-kakitsuke* is thus the "missing link" between Musashi's earlier swordsmanship and what was passed on after his death.

* *Professor Uozumi was able to corroborate that this document was written by Musashi. This translation is based on his findings in Uozumi Takashi,* Miyamoto Musashi: Nihonjin no Michi, *pp. 297–311.*

Having focused intently on the study of combat strategy, I hereby convey in writing the gist of what I have learned. Expressing the Way [of combat strategy] in writing, however, is not something that can be accomplished easily. I will restrict my script to matters in the order in which they come to mind. If you forget the methods for wielding your sword or are unsure on matters of form, read carefully what I have outlined here so as not to deviate from the Way.

(1) About Mindset (心持やうの事)

The mindset required [of the warrior] is to relentlessly deliberate on strategy, whether you are active or sitting down, with others or on your own. You must constantly reflect on this Way. Anticipate how to never lose to others, and with an expansive and straight heart act according to the circumstances within the model of the Way of combat strategy. Work out the mind of others and make sure that they cannot read yours. Do not rely on one thing but be aware of strengths and weaknesses, depths and shallows, leaving nothing to the unexpected. In normal times, and when you meet with the enemy, this mindset is to be maintained, with care taken not to jump to conclusions. Be aware of all things, knowing what is good and bad. This is the mindset for combat strategy.

(2) About Gaze (目付の事)

With regards to where one focuses the eyes, there is only the dual gaze of "looking in" (*kan*) and "looking at" (*ken*). Look carefully at the enemy's face to figure out his heart and intent. When scrutinizing the enemy's face, whether he be near or far, do not think of it as close. Absorb it all as if observing from a distance. Keep your eyes narrower than usual and do not move your eyeballs as you scrutinize him intently and calmly. That way you can see all the movements of his hands and feet and even [what is happening at] his left and right sides. The gaze for "looking at" is gentle whereas that for "looking in" is strong enough to peer into the interior of his heart. You will come to know him well as his heart is reflected in his countenance, which is why you should fix your gaze on the face of each enemy.

(3) About Posture (身なりの事)

You should hold your body in a way that makes you appear big. Your expression should be genial and free of wrinkles. The back of your neck should be slightly toughened, with your shoulders neither strained nor slouching forward. Do not jut out your chest. Project your stomach but do not bend your hips. Your legs should not buckle at the knees, and there should be no distortion in your body. Always strive to preserve this combat posture so that you do not need to change your stance when you encounter the enemy.

(4) About Taking Hold of the Sword (太刀の取やうの事)

When taking hold of the sword, the tips of your forefingers and thumbs should touch, with the forefingers held lightly as if floating. The joint of the thumbs should be fastened [to the hilt], the middle finger should grip slightly tighter, with the ring finger and little finger gripping the strongest. To grip correctly [with the right amount of power in the palms], the fork between the thumbs and forefingers are not forcefully attached to the hilt but should be in line with the back of the sword. The wrists should be flexible and loose, not coiled at all. The hilt should be clasped in a way that the fingers do not touch the sword guard (*tsuba*). The very bottom of the hilt is not to be grasped either. The left and right hands should grip the sword(s) in the same way.

(5) About Footwork (足ぶみの事)

Regarding the movement of your feet, the tips of your toes should glide [lightly] whereas the heels should tread heavily. Types of footwork to be avoided include "jumping feet," "floating feet," "stomping feet," "extracting feet" and "seesaw feet." These are all bad. You have to be able to maneuver unimpeded in [environments such as] mountainous terrain, over rivers and on stony ground. Footwork should not change whether attacking or blocking. Observing how the enemy prepares to strike, it is also very important to stomp with the right foot when attacking. In general, avoid having your stance too wide [by leaving your left foot behind]. The left foot always follows.[1]

(6) About the Five Sword Stances (太刀構五つの事)

1. Enkyoku Tachisuji-no-Koto[2] (一、円極太刀筋之事)

Employed against all sword attacks, the sword pathway of *enkyoku* (middle stance) is broad and is also the most fundamental. The long sword position depends on the enemy and the circumstances. As for the stance itself, the edges of both the left and right swords should not face down or directly to the sides. To keep the enemy at bay, take a position with the long sword tip raised and extended. When you intend to be closer

---

[1] Compare with Article 5 in *Heihō Sanjūgo-kajō*.

[2] This article corresponds with "The Five Exterior Forms"—Number One (*chūdan* = middle stance) in *Gorin-no-sho* (Article 8 in the Water Scroll). It is completely different to the first form of *katsu-totsu kissaki-gaeshi* outlined in *Heihō 39*.

to the enemy, lower the tips slightly and bring the swords nearer your body. When you are thinking of luring the enemy in to attack, lower the swords while keeping them level. When intending to entrap the enemy, or when you have missed the mark, thrust and then, as the enemy tries to strike, pull your long sword back toward your navel with the blade facing down. The target for the thrust is the face and chest. Detach from the enemy's sword and seize him with your hands. There are three cadences for executing return swings of your sword (*kissaki-gaeshi*). If the attack is made with a small strike, return the blade by swinging it around in one [move]. With a large strike, make the ensuing cut a little slower. Delay the return cut when you lunge at your opponent forcefully as if to stomp on his feet. If you cut up at the hands from below, this is the same as the lower stance (*gedan*). Strike up then follow the path for *kissaki-gaeshi* after hitting the target. It is important not to deviate from the sword's pathway.

2. Gidan (二、義断のかまへの事)

With the stance of *gidan* (upper),[3] the right hand should be placed at ear height. The butt of the long sword's hilt should not be splayed [too much from the center], nor should the grip be too tight or overly relaxed. Assume a stance that is facing the front. The short sword in the left hand is held down but not extended, and is pointed in a low, middle or high direction depending on the enemy's stance. The strike itself,

---

[3] Judging by the description, *gidan* is most likely the upper (*jōdan*) stance. This article, therefore, corresponds with "The Five Exterior Forms—Number Two" (*jōdan* = upper stance) in *Gorin-no-sho*, (Article 9 in the Water Scroll), and "Gidan-no-Kamae Jōdan" in *Heihō 39*. As with all of these explanations, the major difference between descriptions of procedures in *Gorin-no-sho* and *Heihō-kakitsuke* is that the former is more general whereas the latter includes detailed technical instruction.

fast or slow, shallow or deep, light or heavy depends on the opponent's attack. The standard target is the enemy's hands. Don't cut down, but in a forward motion. When executing *katsu-totsu*,[4] stand the long sword up, then thrust at and cut the enemy's right hand. Irrespective of whether your swords clash or not, your hands are the same. It is important to strike rapidly. The alternating cut-thrust movement (*katsu-totsu*) can continue [for as long as the opportunity to strike is there]. This [technique] is difficult [to achieve] if you are too close to the enemy. In which case you must win by taking hold of the enemy. Consider this well.

3. Shigeki (三、鷲撃のかまへの事)

There are two ways of employing *shigeki* (lower stance).[5] For the first, extend the tip of the long sword to the front, making sure it does not veer to the left. Attack the enemy at "one-third" of a strike. Lift your hand up as if to execute a blow, then thrust instead, being sure to avoid the tip of the enemy's sword. If you have the mind to knock his sword down, strike quickly and then return your hands slowly. In either case, be ready to revert to *kissaki-gaeshi*. Another way of executing *shigeki* is to direct your sword tip at the enemy while lowering your hand to place it on your right leg. Strike the enemy the instant you sense his intention to act. The shallowness or depth, lightness or heaviness of your strike will depend on the enemy's spirit. This requires much contemplation.

---

[4] See Article 31 in the Water Scroll.

[5] This third procedure corresponds with "The Five Exterior Forms—Number Three" (*gedan* = lower stance) in *Gorin-no-sho* (Article 10 in the Water Scroll). In *Heihō 39* it is the fourth technique (written as 重気), *shigeki-no-kamae*, *hidari-waki* [left-side stance].

4. Uchoku (四、迂直のかまへの事)

With *uchoku*,[6] assume the left-side stance (*hidari-waki*), with the long sword (right hand) at the left and the short sword (left hand) not raised high, making sure your arms are not crossed too deeply. Parry the enemy's strike [from below] the first third of the way through. If you are of a mind to knock his sword down, evade his strike to your left hand by lowering it slightly with a cutting motion, then counter-cut him diagonally [from above] with the right. It is important to strike quickly. Make sure the line of the blade is true as you swing around to strike with *katsu-totsu* and *kissaki-gaeshi*.

5. Suikei (五、水形のかまへの事)

With *suikei*,[7] the tip of the long sword should not be open to the side, and the left hand (short sword) is thrust out. The left and right arms are held open on each side of the chest, but are not straightened at the elbows. When the enemy launches

---

[6] In *Heihō 39*, this is called *uchoku-no-kamae migi-waki* [right-side stance]. In *Gorin-no-sho*, it is "The Five Exterior Forms—Number Four" (*hidari-waki* = left-side stance) (Article 11 in the Water Scroll). Uozumi surmises that it is likely Terao Kumenosuke made a mistake when transcribing/remembering the techniques in the additional four articles that he added to *Heihō 35*. In Musashi's original manuscript of *Heihō-kakitsuke*, he writes *u-choku* in syllabic Japanese script instead of *kanji*. "U" is an *on* reading for the ideogram for "right" (右), which apparently resulted in some confusion when Kumenosuke wrote that it was for the "right-side stance." After all, it was twenty years after Musashi's death when Kumenosuke added the four articles to make *Heihō 39*. This has resulted in substantial difficulty in fitting the pieces of Musashi's technical puzzle together. It has also provoked a certain degree of animosity among adherents of the Niten Ichi-ryū schools over the last three and a half centuries, with differing interpretations of their founder's ideas.

[7] In *Heihō 39*, this is still called *suikei-no-kamae* but is the stance assumed to be *gedan* (lower stance). In *Gorin-no-sho*, it is "The Five Exterior Forms—Number Five" (*migi-waki* = right-side stance) described in Article 12 in the Water Scroll.

his attack, cross past his sword as you strike up his centerline to forehead height [into *jōdan*]. The aim is to cut broadly to the front. Do not allow the blade to keep going through to the left. Follow through and swing around with the *kissaki-gaeshi* movement. Depending on the circumstances, you may assume *uchoku* (left-side stance). This needs to be decided in an instant.

Generally, these are the only five sword paths for striking the enemy. There is only one way to cut with a sword [and is in line with these paths]. Be mindful of this.

(7) About Hitting and Striking[8] (当ルと云ト打ト云事)

Hitting is not meant to be a winning strike. Hitting has its own principle. You hit to weaken the enemy and make him act irrationally. Striking, on the other hand, is executed with certainty [and killing in mind]. Consider this carefully.

(8) Hitting the Hands (手に当る事)

There are eight opportunities to hit the hands:
1. First, hit with the "one-count" cadence.[9]
2. Second, slap and hit from *gedan* (lower stance).
3. Third, hit [just as he moves] when you lower the swords.
4. Fourth, facing off in *chūdan* (middle stance), place your long sword on top, then hit with a timing slightly askew from the "one-count" cadence.
5. Fifth, in the same stance, place your long sword underneath and hit.

---

[8] See Article 12 in *Heihō Sanjūgo-kajō*.
[9] See Article 14 in the Water Scroll.

6. Sixth, hit as the enemy blocks.
7. Seventh, hit from a block.
8. Eighth, when the enemy slaps your strike away, follow through with the long sword and hit.

These are the designated points for hitting. Do not despair if your hit misses the mark. Just realize that your rhythm is wrong.

(9) Hitting the Legs (足に当る事)

There are six opportunities to hit the legs:
1. First, when the enemy blocks.
2. Second, when the enemy tries to deflect your sword.
3. Third, when the enemy assumes a right-side stance.
4. Fourth, when your sword has been hit down.
5. Fifth, when the enemy has a long sword and assumes the *kasumi*[10] stance, revert to the *chūdan* (middle) position and hit his legs.
6. Sixth, when the enemy is in the *chūdan* stance, come from below and strike his legs as you affix your short sword to his sword [to suppress it].

These are the six points for striking[11] the legs.

---

[10] A stance seen in various schools of swordsmanship in which the sword is held horizontally with the hilt around head height, the cutting edge facing up and the tip pointed at the adversary.

[11] Musashi uses the verb *utsu* ("to strike") instead of *ataru* ("to hit"). It may seem trivial, but it does cause confusion considering Musashi makes a clear distinction between hitting and striking.

(10) About Blocking (うくると云事)

In the case of blocking:[12]

1. First, affix your sword as the enemy attacks and let it slide off.[13] Cadence is very important.
2. Second, as the opponent strikes, point the tip of your long sword to the region extending from the right hand to the right eye to block by thrusting the tip into the oncoming blow.

With both blocks, it is important that the movement is not an upward one. The hands are lifted to a higher position as if to thrust forward into the attack [not from underneath].

3. Also, when the enemy is close, you can receive [his attack] by pulling back and counter-striking quickly [with the other sword].

These are the three blocks.

(11) About Moving in Close[14] (入身の位の事)

1. First, block as the enemy attacks and move in close as if to pass through him.
2. Second, when the opponent blocks, affix your sword to his and move in.
3. Third, when the enemy is holding his sword to the right side, or when you hit his legs, or when he is about to block or strike, pivot your body and enter his space.

---

[12] Compare with Article 28 in the Water Scroll.

[13] This entry is problematic as there are two possibilities for the reading of one of the characters. It could read as *u-ke-n* ("enemy's block") instead of *u-ta-n* ("enemy's strike"). "Receive the opponent's strike with your sword and elude [by letting it slide off]."

[14] Compare with Article 26 in the Water Scroll.

4. Fourth, enter when your rhythm is not synchronized with the enemy's.

In all cases, it is bad to hunch your back and stick out your arms when moving in close. Pivot forward into a side-on stance[15] and stick close to the enemy. When you enter, be sure you are completely inside. Also, ensure that your line [to cut] is straight, your body is not inclined in the slightest and your movement is powerful. Study this well.

(12) Cadences for Striking the Enemy (敵を打拍子の事)

There are various cadences for striking with the sword.[16] The striking rhythm called "one-count" (itsu-byōshi) is to not let your will manifest in your body and mind and strike from the void. Striking from nothing, you deliver a blow at a place your opponent does not expect. This is the "one-count" striking cadence. The enemy is also competing against your spirit and while preparing to attack, strike unexpectedly. This is called an "empty strike" and is a crucial tactic. The "delayed cadence" (okure-byōshi) involves leaving your body and spirit behind when [seemingly] delivering the blow, and then landing the [real] strike when your enemy hesitates. This is what is meant by "delayed cadence." With the "flint spark" blow (sekka, or hishi-bi), have the intention to slide up the enemy's sword with lightning speed. It must be executed powerfully and fast with every bone and sinew of your body in unison. This should be studied. With the "autumn leaves" strike (momiji), the opponent's sword is struck down with speed and force as you affix your sword to his. Even if you do not strike his sword, it is difficult for him to pass [with your sword in his position on his].

---

[15] Hitoemi, or minimized profile facing the opponent.

[16] See Articles 14–20 in the Water Scroll and Article 22 in Heihō Sanjūgo-kajō.

With the "flowing water" strike, attack the enemy in spirit and body as one with one blow, but deliver the long sword calmly and obstinately. There are also several timings for striking at the start, middle and end [of the movement].

(13) About Taking the Initiative (先のかけやうの事)

There are various ways for "taking the initiative."[17] What is known as *ken-no-sen* (crackdown initiative)[18] is when you instigate an attack on the enemy in order to win. *Tai-no-sen* (cleanup initiative)[19] is employed when the opponent attacks. You must modify the timing of the initiative [and strike afterwards]. This requires careful scrutiny. With *tai-tai-no-sen* (coinciding initiative),[20] both you and the enemy attack each other simultaneously, but you must override his rhythm. Or, there is the initiative employed when your attacking initiative coincides with that of your opponent. Make a sudden change to force your initiative over his. There is also the initiative in which you seize victory by taking your time [slowing things down] when both you and the enemy are brimming in spirit. There are initiatives of a "weak and strong," "light and heavy," "shallow and deep" mind. Then there is the "case-by-case" initiative and the "vocal" initiative. These should all be studied.

---

[17] See Article 2 in the Fire Scroll and Article 13 in *Heihō Sanjūgo-kajō*. Musashi had written of the importance of taking the "initiative" (*sen*) in the *Heidōkyō*, but it was from *Heihō Sanjūgo-kajō* that he divided them into three variants.

[18] Literally "attacking initiative."

[19] Literally "waiting initiative."

[20] Literally "body-body initiative."

(14) About Shouting (声をかくると云事)

To shout at your opponent does not mean that you are yelling all the time. You should not shout in time with your striking rhythm. Shouts are made before and after the fact. When it is uncertain where you will attack, then it is feasible to let out a cry beforehand. There is also the post-attack cry in which you bellow after delivering a blow. This is the "after shout." There is the shout *Ei*, which can be made loudly or quietly. There is also the shout *Maitta*. It depends on the [situation surrounding the] attack. An "accompanying" shout, which is tied to a strike when both rhythms are similar, is *Ya*, and is for overriding the opponent's cadence. This shout is made inside the mouth, in your heart so that nobody can hear it. These are the three cries of "before," "after" and "within."

It may seem that shouting is unnecessary. Nevertheless, as we shout against the wind, waves, and fire on the battlefield, we must also shout down [the enemy's] vitality. Do not cry out at night. Judge each situation [on its own merits].

The above articles are meant as an outline. Train hard to master each. This is the way to practice combat strategy. Supplementary details shall be documented in other writings.

Auspicious Day, 11th Month, Kan'ei 15 (1638)
Shinmen Musashi Genshin

"Senki" (Fighting Spirit) written by Musashi
(Print in author's collection)

COMBAT STRATEGY IN 35 ARTICLES

HEIHŌ SANJŪGO-KAJŌ

兵法三十五箇条

Main Points

* Heihō Sanjūgo-kajō *means "Combat Strategy in 35 Articles," although it contains 36 articles altogether.*[1]

* *Musashi wrote* Heihō Sanjūgo-kajō *in 1641 and presented it to Hosokawa Tadatoshi, lord of the Hosokawa domain in Kumamoto. As such, the tone of the text is honorific.*

* *Musashi was probably motivated to write his text because Yagyū Munenori of the Yagyū Shinkage-ryū school of swordsmanship had presented Tadatoshi with his celebrated treatise,* Heihō Kadensho, *four years earlier.*

* Heihō Sanjūgo-kajō *serves as a supplement to* Gorin-no-sho *in terms of content. It is useful to compare both to gain a fuller understanding of Musashi's swordsmanship.*

* *In 1666, Musashi's student Terao Magonojō added four more articles and produced an extended version known as* Heihō Sanjūkyu-kajō. *This was used instead of* Gorin-no-sho *a transmission scroll in the Kumamoto lineage of* Niten Ichi-ryū.

---

[1] The Shimada copy of this document is titled *Enmei-ryū Sanjūgo-kajō.*

* *If the article containing the four descriptions of technical procedures is counted as four instead of one, the total is 42. Thus,* Heihō 39 *is also referred to by some as* Heihō Yonjū-ni-kajō (42).

* *The source for this translation and observations is Uozumi Takashi's* Miyamoto Musashi: Nihonjin no Michi, *pp. 325–33*

* *The sections that Kumenosuke added are marked with △ (39-X).*

Introduction

I humbly commit to paper for the first time[2] the methods of the Heihō Nitō Ichi-ryū school of combat strategy which I have developed through many years of training. Considering the intended recipient of this text, it is difficult to express the content adequately in words. It concerns the way one must control the sword in the style one normally practices. I will record the principle elements of this as they come to mind.

---

[2] Musashi had already written *Heidōkyō* and *Heihō-kakitsuke* for his students. *Heihō Sanjūgo-kajō* was written specifically for Hosokawa Tadatoshi, a student of Yagyū Shinkage-ryū, so the tone of the introduction is very polite and his statement claiming this was his first work is meant as a sign of humility. Notice that at this juncture Musashi was still referring to his school as Nitō Ichi-ryū (School of Two Swords as One). Lord Tadatoshi had received *Heihō Kadensho* (1632) from Yagyū Munenori in 1637. It was he who requested Musashi write for him a similar text on his school. It is unclear whether Tadatoshi ever read the text as he died about one month after Musashi presented it to him. Musashi's trusted disciple, Terao Kumenosuke, the younger brother of Magonojō, got hold of the text (either the original or a copy in Musashi's hand). In copying the text himself, Kumenosuke omitted Article 15 but added four more articles which he took from *Heihō-kakitsuke* and *Gorin-no-sho*. In particular, the section explaining the techniques, apart from the first one, is taken from *Heihō-kakitsuke*. Musashi did not include technical explanations but Kumenosuke did as he intended to use the 39 Articles as a transmission scroll for his own students. This version by Kumenosuke is called *Heihō Sanjūkyū-kajō* (*Heihō in 39 Articles*). It is also sometimes referred to as *Heihō Shijōni-kajō* (*Heihō in 42 Articles*). The discrepancy comes from what are counted as articles.

(1) Why I Name My Way that of "Two Swords"
(一、此道二刀と名付事)

I call this Way that of "Two Swords" as we train with a sword in each hand. The left hand is considered of less importance as followers aim to master wielding the long sword with one hand. Learning to wield the sword with one hand is advantageous when in battle formation, while riding a horse, traversing marshes, rivers, narrow paths an d rocky surfaces, running, and in a crowd. If you are holding something in your left hand and it is difficult [to brandish the sword with both hands], the sword is operated with [the right] one. A sword held in one hand will feel heavy at first but later you will be able to manipulate it freely. For example, learning to shoot a bow increases strength, and the power for riding horses also comes through training. In terms of the skills of common people, the sailor develops strength through working the rudder and oars. The farmer gains power through using his plow and hoe. You will cultivate strength also through taking up the sword. Nevertheless, it is best to use a sword that suits your physical capabilities.[3]

(2) About Understanding the Way of Combat
(一、兵法之道見立処之事)

The principles of this Way are the same for both large-scale and small-scale strategy. What I write here is for small-scale strategy, but if the task of a general is kept in mind, his arms and legs correspond to his vassals and his torso to his foot soldiers and subjects. It is in this way that the country is governed as if it were a person's body. As such, large- and small-scale conflict is no different in the Way of combat strategy. When

---

[3] This section corresponds with Article 5 in the Earth Scroll.

practicing strategy, the whole body must be employed as one, devoid of surplus and deficiency, neither too strong nor too weak, with the spirit circulating evenly from head to toe.[4]

(3) About How to Take Hold of the Sword
(一、太刀取様之事)

To take hold of the sword, the forefinger and thumb should brush [the hilt] lightly, while the middle finger should hold with medium strength and the ring and little finger grip tightly. As with the sword, there is also "life" and "death" in one's hands. When assuming a fighting stance, parrying or blocking, the hand that forgets about cutting and stops is said to be "dead." The hand that lives is one that moves in harmony with the sword at any time without becoming rigid and is at ease to cut well. This is called the "live" hand. The wrists should not be entwined, the elbows neither too taut nor too bent, the upper muscles of the arms relaxed and the lower muscles tensed. Study this well.[5]

(4) About Posture (一、身のかゝりの事)

One's posture should be such that the face is not tilted down, nor should it be raised too high. The shoulders are neither tensed nor slouched. The abdomen should be pushed forward but not the chest. One should not bend at the hips. The knees are not locked. The body faces straight ahead so that it appears to be broad. "Combat posture in everyday life; Everyday posture in combat." Consider this carefully.[6]

---

[4] This article is addressed in more detail in the Fire Scroll.

[5] Compare with Article 4 in the Water Scroll.

[6] Compare with Article 2, Water Scroll.

(5) About Footwork⁷ (一、足ぶみの事)

Use of the feet depends on the situation. There are big and small, slow and fast ways of stepping, the same as when you normally walk. Footwork to avoid includes "jumping feet," "floating feet," "stomping feet," "extracting feet" and "seesaw feet." Notwithstanding the ease or difficulty of footwork wherever you are, be sure to move with confidence. You will learn more about this in a later section.⁸

(6) About Gaze (一、目付之事)

With regards to "fixing one's gaze," although many methods have been advocated in the past, these days it usually means that the eyes are directed at the [enemy's] face. The eyes are fixed in such a way that they are slightly narrower than normal and [the enemy is] observed calmly. The eyeballs do not move, and when the enemy encroaches, no matter how close, the eyes appear to look into the distance. With such a gaze, to say nothing of the enemy's techniques, you will also be able to see both sides as well. Observe with the dual gaze of "looking in" (*kan*) and "looking at" (*ken*)—stronger with *kan* and weaker with *ken*. Use of the eyes can also communicate intent to the enemy. Intentions are to be revealed in the eyes, but not the mind. This should be examined carefully.⁹

---

⁷ The title is similar to Article 5, Water Scroll, but the content is introduced in Article 7 of the Wind Scroll, albeit with some variation in the explanations of flawed footwork.

⁸ It appears that Musashi intended to write more on this topic. He does elaborate in *Gorin-no-sho* but does not go into further detail in this document. Perhaps he was aware that the intended reader, Hosokawa Tadatoshi, would take it as an affront to the Yagyū Shinkage-ryū style of swordsmanship that he was studying.

⁹ Compare with Article 3, Water Scroll.

△ **(39-1) About the Five-Way Stances**
(一、五方の構の次第)

1. *Katsu-totsu Kissaki-gaeshi, Jōdan* (Upper stance)
2. *Gidan, Chūdan* (Middle stance)
3. *Shigeki, Hidari-waki* (Left-side stance)
4. *Uchoku, Migi-waki* (Right-side stance)
5. *Suikei, Gedan* (Lower stance)

(Refer to the corresponding section in *Heihō-kakitsuke*.)

(7) About Measuring the Interval[10] (一、間積りの事)

There are various theories in other disciplines when it comes to *ma* (timing and interval). I am only concerned here with combat strategy.[11] Whatever the Way, the more you train the more you will realize [that the mind should not be fixed in one place]. Basically, when you are at an interval where your sword can strike the enemy, you should think that the enemy's sword can also reach you.[12] Forget your body when you are set to kill your opponent.[13] Examine this carefully.

(8) About Mindset (心持之事)

One's mind should neither dwindle nor be in an excited state. It must not be rueful nor afraid. It is straight and expansive,

---

[10] This section is not found in *Gorin-no-sho*.

[11] Musashi is stating that the distance in which you can strike your opponent means that the enemy can also strike you.

[12] In the fencing terminology of medieval Europe, this is called "Just Distance," that is, the interval where, if you are close enough to strike your opponent, he is close enough to strike you.

[13] This article is somewhat difficult to decipher but considered in the context as advice to Tadatoshi, it may be addressing teachings in Yagyū Shinkage-ryū about gauging an advantageous (safe) interval for you over the enemy.

with one's "heart of intent" faint and one's "heart of perception" substantial. The mind is like water, able to respond aptly to changing situations. Water can be a sparkling hue of emerald green, it can be a single drop or a blue ocean. This should be carefully studied.

(9) To Know the Upper, Middle and Lower Levels of Strategy (兵法上中下の位を知る事)

Stances are adopted in combat, but a show of various sword positions in order to appear strong or fast is regarded as lower-level strategy. Further, refined-looking strategy, flaunting an array of techniques and rhythmical mastery to give the impression of beauty and magnificence, is regarded as middle level. Upper-level strategy looks neither strong nor weak, not irregular, not fast, not glorious and not bad. It looks broad, direct and serene. Examine this carefully.[14]

(10) About the "Cord-Measure" (いとかねと云事)

Always hold a cord-measure in your mind. By holding the cord against each opponent to size him up, you will see his strengths, weaknesses, straightness, crookedness, and tense and relaxed points. With your mind's measure, pull the cord, making it straight so that you can quantify the enemy's heart. With this measure, you should be able to know the round, uneven, long, short, crooked or straight features of the enemy. This must be studied.

---

[14] A corresponding article is not included in *Gorin-no-sho*.

(11) About "Sword Pathways" (太刀之道之事)

Not knowing the pathway of the sword inside out make it difficult to brandish your weapon as you like. Furthermore, if [the sword swings are] not decisive,[15] or you do not bear in mind the back and side of the sword blade, or if the sword is used [to chop] like a knife or rice spatula, it will be difficult to enter the frame of mind needed to cut the enemy down. Train to strike your opponent effectively, always thinking about the sword's pathway, and wield it calmly as if it were a heavy weapon.[16]

(12) About "Striking and Hitting" (打くあたると云事)

The methods of striking (*utsu*) and hitting (*ataru*) are both used in swordsmanship. Learning to strike your target with conviction through test cutting[17] and the like will enable you to strike as you please. When you cannot work out a way to make a decisive strike, hit the enemy any way you can. If the hit connects, even with force, it will never count as a strike. Do not be concerned if you hit the enemy's body or his sword, or even if you miss altogether. Just be mindful of preparing your hands and feet for a true strike. This must be practiced dutifully.

(13) About the "Three Initiatives" (三ツの先と云事)

Of the "three initiatives" (*sen*), the first one involves attacking the enemy first.[18] The second is the initiative taken when your opponent attacks you.[19] The third is when you and the enemy

---

[15] This can also be translated as a separate sentence: "Moreover, [the cuts] will not be strong."

[16] Compare with Article 7, Water Scroll.

[17] Refer to note 4, Wind Scroll.

[18] In other words, when you initiate the attack.

[19] When the opponent initiates an attack.

attack simultaneously. Your body must be primed to attack first, but strike keeping your legs and spirit centered without being too relaxed or tense, thereby unsettling the enemy. This is *ken-no-sen*, the "crackdown initiative." Next, when the enemy attacks you, have no concern for your body, but when the distance is close, free your mind and seize the initiative from the enemy as you follow his movement. When you and the enemy attack at the same time, keep your body strong and straight and take the initiative with your sword, body, legs and spirit. Seizing the initiative is of the essence.

(14) About "Traversing Critical Points" (渡をこすと云事)

In a situation where you and your opponent are in position to hit each other, you should attack. If you want to move past the critical point, advance with your body and legs and stick to him. There is nothing to fear once you have passed the critical point. This should be considered carefully with reference to my future teachings.

(15) On "Body Replaces Sword" (一、太刀にかはる身の事) (Absent in *Heihō 39*)

"Body replaces sword" means that when you strike with the sword your body should not be connected to it. When he sees your body attacking, he should then see your sword landing. Moreover, it is the same mindset of "sword replaces body." Keep an empty mind and never strike with sword, body and spirit simultaneously. Examine carefully the notion of mind and body within [within the sword stroke].

(16) About the "Two Steps" (一、二ツの足と云事)

"Two steps"[20] refers to moving both feet in delivering a sword stroke. When you ride or release the enemy's sword, or when you maneuver forward or back, you make two steps. It feels as if your feet are connected. If you make only one step when striking,[21] you will be stuck on the spot. Thought of as a pair, this is just like normal walking. This needs to be examined carefully.

(17) About "Trampling the Sword" (一、剣をふむと云事)

This is to tread on the enemy's sword tip with your left foot just as his sword is swung down. If you seize the initiative with your sword, body and mind as you trample on his sword, victory will be yours. Without this mindset, the encounter will degenerate into a tit-for-tat exchange. Your feet will be fine as you will not stamp on the sword all that often. Consider this well.

(18) About "Arresting the Shadow" (一、陰をおさゆると云)

"Arresting the shadow" (*yin*) means to carefully observe your enemy in order to know if his mind is overly engaged and where it is lacking. Pointing your sword when his mind is preoccupied and diverting his attention, then arresting the shadow of the area that is lacking will upset his rhythm and victory will be for the taking. Even so, it is crucial that you do not leave your mind on the shadow and forget to strike. You must work this out.[22]

---

[20] This is the same teaching as *yin-yang* footwork in Article 5, Water Scroll.

[21] In other words, if you step out as you cut but leave your back foot behind without snapping it up.

[22] This teaching is essentially to capture the opponent's intention to circumvent his attack. The *yin* shadow is invisible.

(19) About "Shifting the Shadow" (一、影を動かすと云事)

This shadow is that of *yang*. When the enemy pulls his sword back and assumes a front-on stance,[23] suppress his sword with your mind and make your body empty. As soon the enemy encroaches, unleash with your sword. This will surely make him move. When he does, it is easy to win. This method did not exist before. Do not allow the mind to become fixed as you strike at protruding parts of his body. Ponder this carefully.[24]

(20) About "Detaching the Bowstring" (一、弦をはづすと云事)

"Detaching the bowstring" is employed when your mind and the enemy's are tightly connected [with a bowstring]. In such a situation, you must promptly detach [the string] with your body, sword, legs and mind. Detaching is most effective when the enemy least expects it. This should be explored.

(21) About the "Small Comb" Teaching (一、小櫛のおしへの事)

The spirit of the "small comb" is to untangle knots. Hold a comb in your mind and use it to slash threads in the enemy's web of entanglement. Entangling with threads and pulling strings are similar. Pulling is stronger, however, as entanglement is a tactic executed with a weaker mind. This should be considered judiciously.

---

[23] As in *wakigamae* or other fighting stances that conceal the sword.

[24] This means to make the opponent change his tactic. With these two articles in *Heihō Sanjūgo-kajō*, the *yin* and *yang* shadows are the reverse of how they are described in *Gorin-no-sho*.

(22) About "Knowing Gaps in Cadence"
（一、拍子の間を知ると云事）

"Knowing gaps in cadence" depends on the enemy. The cadence of each enemy is different. Some are fast and some are slow. With an opponent who is slow, do not move your body and conceal the start of your sword movement, quickly delivering a blow out of nothing. This is the rhythm of "one-count" (*itsu-byōshi*).[25]

With a fast opponent, feign an attack with your body and mind and strike your opponent down after he responds. This rhythm is called the "two-phase traversing cadence" (*ni-no-koshi*).

The cadence of "no-thought no-form" (*munen-musō*) requires having your body primed to strike while holding your spirit and your sword back. As soon as you see a gap in your opponent's spirit, strike forcefully from nothing. This is the cadence of "no-thought no-form."

"Delayed cadence" (*okure-byōshi*) is a rhythm employed when your opponent is ready to slap or parry your attack. Ever so slowly, strike at the opening revealed [by him in his movement]. This is "Delayed cadence" [and the enemy will miss as a result]. Practice this rhythm diligently.

(23) About "Stopping the Start" （一、枕のおさへと云事）

"Stopping the start" is employed when you sense the enemy is about to attack. Suppress the start just as he is thinking about striking, before it can take form. Use your mind, body and sword to muzzle the strike. When you sense his intent, it is the perfect time to strike first, or to enter his space, for breaking

---

[25] This can also be pronounced as *ichi-byōshi, ichi-hyōshi, ippyōshi* or *hitotsu-hyōshi*.

away and for seizing the initiative. It can be employed in all situations. Train in this judiciously.

△ **(39-2) About "Making it Bind"**
(A simplified version of Article 26 in the Water Scroll of *Gorin-no-sho* [Scroll 2].)

(24) About "Knowing the Conditions"
(一、景気を知ると云事)

"Knowing the conditions" means to carefully ascertain the ebbs and flows, shallows and depths, weaknesses and strengths of the location and the enemy. By always utilizing the teaching of the "cord-measure" [10 above], such conditions can be sensed immediately. By catching the conditions of the moment, you will be victorious whether facing the front or the rear. Ponder this carefully.

(25) About "Becoming your Enemy" (一、敵に成と云事)

You should think of your own body as the enemy's. Whether the opponent is holed up somewhere or is a mighty force,[26] or you come face to face with an expert in the martial Way, you must anticipate the difficulties going through his mind. If you cannot calculate the confusion in his mind, you will mistake his weaknesses for strengths, see a novice as an accomplished master, view a small enemy as a powerful one, or grant your foe advantages when he has none. Become your enemy. Study this well.

---

[26] Literally a "large enemy," this could be referring to an unusually big man (as Musashi at 5 ft. 9 in. (182 cm) purportedly was), or a force of many opponents.

(26) "Retained Mind" and "Freed Mind"
(一、残心放心の事)

"Retained mind" (*zanshin*) and "freed mind" (*hōshin*) should be employed as the circumstance and moment dictates. When you take up your sword, it is standard for the "heart of intent" (*i-no-kokoro*) to be freed and the "heart of perception" (*shin-no-kokoro*) to be retained (kept hold of). The moment you strike at the enemy, release your "heart of perception" and retain your "heart of intent." There are various methods for employing "retained mind" and "freed mind." This should be studied carefully.

(27) About "Opportunity Knocks" (一、縁のあたりと云事)

"Opportunity knocks" is when the enemy comes in close to attack you with his sword and you either slap it away with your own sword, parry the attack or hit. In all cases of slapping, parrying or hitting, the enemy's attack should be considered an opportunity. If actions of riding, evading or sticking to the enemy's sword are all executed with the intention of striking, your body, mind and sword will always be primed to deliver. Carefully consider this.

(28) About "Sticking Like Lacquer and Glue"
(一、しつかうのつきと云事)

"Sticking like lacquer and glue" means to get in very close to the enemy. Stick steadfastly to the enemy with your legs, hips and face, leaving no gaps, just like bonding with lacquer and glue. If there are any gaps, the enemy will have the freedom to apply various techniques. The cadence for moving in to stick to the enemy is the same as "stopping the start" and is executed with a serene state of mind.

(29) About the "Body of an Autumn Monkey"
(一、しうこうの身と云事)

The "body of an autumn monkey" means that when you stick to an enemy's body, you must do it as if you had no arms. The worst way to attempt this is to leave your body back as you stretch your arms out. If you just extend your arms, your body will lag behind. Using the area from your left shoulder down to the forearm is advantageous in an attack, but never resort to only using your hands. The cadence for sticking to the enemy is the same as [in 28] above.

(30) About "Contesting Height" (一、たけくらべと云事)

"Contesting height" is employed when very close and clinging to the enemy. Make yourself as tall as you can, as if contesting height. In your mind, make yourself taller than your opponent. The cadence for getting in close is the same as the others. Consider this well.

(31) About the "Door" Teaching (一、扉のおしへと云事)

The body of the "door"[27] is used when moving in to stick to the enemy. Make the span of your body wide and straight as if to conceal the enemy's sword and body. Fuse yourself to the enemy so that there is no space between your bodies. Then pivot to the side, making yourself slender and straight, and smash your shoulder into his chest to knock him down. Practice this.

---

[27] The word Musashi uses for door is *toboso*. Written with a different ideogram, *toboso* also means "pivot hinge."

(32) The "General and His Troops" Teaching
(一、将卒のおしへの事)

The "general and his troops" is a teaching that means once you embody the principles of strategy, you see the enemy as your troops and yourself as their general. Do not allow the enemy any freedom whatsoever, neither permitting him to swing nor thrust with his sword. He is so completely under your sway that he is unable to think of any tactics. This is crucial.

(33) About the "Stance of No-Stance"
(一、うかゞうむかうと云事)

The "stance of no-stance" refers to [the mindset] when you are holding your sword. You can adopt various stances, but if your mind is so preoccupied with the *engarde* position, the sword and your body will be ineffectual. Even though you always have your sword, do not become preoccupied with any particular stance. There are three varieties of upper stance (*jōdan*) as well as three attitudes for the middle (*chūdan*) and lower (*gedan*) stances that you can adopt. The same can be said for the left-side and right-side stances (*hidari-waki* and *migi-waki*). Seen as such, this is the mind of no-stance. Ponder this carefully.

△ (39-3) About "Assessing the Location"
△ (39-4) About "Dealing to Many Enemies"

(Simplified versions of Article 1 in the Fire Scroll [Scroll 3] and Article 33 in the Water Scroll [Scroll 2] of *Gorin-no-Sho*.)

(34) About "The Body of a Boulder"
（一、いわをの身と云事）

"The body of a boulder" is to have an unmovable mind that is strong and vast. You come to embody myriad principles through your training, to the extent that nothing can touch you. All living things will avoid you. Although devoid of consciousness, even plants will not take root on a boulder. Even the rain and wind will do nothing to a boulder. You must strive to understand what this "body" means.

(35) To "Know the Moment" （一、期をしる事）

To "know the moment" is to know opportunities that come quickly and those that come later. It is to know when to retreat and when to engage. In my school, there is an essential sword teaching called "Direct Transmission" (*Jikitsū*). The particulars of this will be conveyed orally.

(36)[28] About "Myriad Principles, One Void"
（一、万理一空の事）

Although myriad principles return to the Ether, this is all but impossible to explain in writing. I humbly suggest that you contemplate this concept yourself.

---

[28] Although titled "Combat Strategy in 35 Articles," here is number 36. It is perfectly plausible that Musashi simply miscounted or perhaps he did not consider the final entry developed enough to count as a definitive article. Maybe the title "Myriad Principles, One Void" is meant as a conclusion.

The 35 articles prescribed above outline my views on the mindset of strategy and how it is to be approached. Some of the entries may seem deficient but they concern things I have already imparted to you. I have refrained from writing about my school's sword techniques as I will teach them directly. Should there be any entries you are unsure of, please allow me to explain in person.

An auspicious day, 2nd Month of Kan'ei 18 (1641)[29]
Shinmen Musashi Genshin

39-5. [Postscript in *Heihō 39*]

(Written on the fifteenth day of the 8th month of Kanbun 6 [1666] by Terao Kumenosuke.)

---

[29] The recipient, Lord Hosokawa Tadatoshi, became ill on the eighteenth day of the first month. Musashi presented the document to him as a certificate concluding his training, but he passed away on the seventeenth day of the third month.

Memorial of state of Musashi near the Reigando Cave in Kumamoto.

THE FIVE-DIRECTION SWORD PATHWAYS

GOHŌ-NO-TACHIMICHI
五 方 之 太 刀 道

Main Points

* *This was written by Musashi as the original introduction to*
  Gorin-no-sho *(Scrolls 1–5 above).*

* *It was used by Musashi's direct student, Terao Kumenosuke, as
  a transmission scroll in* Kumamoto's Niten Ichi-ryū.

* *The original was written entirely in* kanbun *(Chinese script).*

* *Musashi asked a local monk in Kumamoto to proof his script. It
  was subsequently rewritten by Musashi but he had a change of
  heart and decided not to include it in* Gorin-no-sho. *It seemed
  too ostentatious and he preferred instead to leave everything
  in standard Japanese without referencing the Chinese classics.*

* *This translation and observations are based on Uozumi Takashi's
  research in* Miyamoto Musashi: Nihonjin no Michi, *pp. 325–33.*

Combat strategy (*heihō*) is a Way. Therefore, attaining the principles [for victory] when crossing swords with the enemy is also applicable on the field [of battle] of the "Three Armies."[1] Why should it be differentiated? Furthermore, victory is not decided by fighting the enemy you face. The victor is already determined before the fight even begins so there is no need to wait for commencement. The Way of combat strategy must be pursued always with no deviation. The laws of strategy are to be followed, but not blindly. Even secrets cannot be hidden. Carrying it through will reveal many things. When engaged in a difficult contest, wait [until the right time comes]. You can strike the hanging bell only when you are deep inside the temple building. [So, to to become accomplished in the Way of combat strategy you must train hard and enter the depths.]

From ancient times, there have been several dozen traditions in Japan expounding their own methods for pursuing the art [of swordsmanship]. What they consider to be their Way, however, is comprised of rough tactics centered on brute strength, or a preference for gentleness instead with the focus placed on trivial principles. Or, they may depend only on long swords or have a proclivity for short swords. They invent a multitude of flawed procedures (stances and forms) and label them *omote* (surface) and *oku* (interior). Alas, there cannot be two Ways. Why is it [when making various claims] they keep making the same mistakes? Those who promote false Ways to gain fame and fortune do as they please, flaunting their "skills" to deceive the world. That they win is only because they choose less skilled opponents to fight. It is like somebody with a smattering of ability defeating somebody with none whatsoever. It is totally wrong to refer to it as a [universal] discipline

---

[1] The term "Three Armies" refers to the vanguard, middle guard and rear guard. In other words, it is a synonym for a "great army."

and there is nothing that can be taken from it.

I have immersed my spirit [into the Way of combat strategy], honed my inner thoughts [in training] for a long time and finally mastered this Way.

The warrior must always carry two swords in his daily life, one long and one short. As such, it is fundamental to know how to use both. This is like having the sun and the moon in the heavens. I have laid down that there are five ways to hold the sword (upper, middle, lower, left side and right side). This is like the five stars (Jupiter, Mars, Venus, Mercury and Saturn) that occupy the skies around the Polaris. Just as the five stars rotate and the months pass by [in an orderly fashion], anything that contravenes that order is challenged and rejected. There are five sword stances (*kamae*): *jōdan* (upper), *chūdan* (middle), *gedan* (lower), *hidari-waki* (left side) and *migi-waki* (right side). Each one has meaning [as an effective stance] depending on the situation. This is different from other schools promoting their various *omote* and *oku* procedures. When I engage in a fight, I draw both of my swords immediately. If I only have a short sword and no long sword, then I will fight with that. If I do not have a short sword, then I will resort to using my bare hands. One way or another, I will be victorious. Depending on the circumstances, a large sword [equal in length to the space between your outstretched arms] might not be sufficient, whereas a short one [the length of your thumb] might well be. There are times when you need to initiate the attack against a strong enemy. At other times you should hold back and wait for the right moment, even though the enemy is weak. Avoid prejudices and base your action on the time and circumstances, maintaining your "center" [so that you can respond to anything freely]. The "center" is the "Universally Correct Way." The center is precisely what the Way of combat strategy that I stand for is based on.

A person once proclaimed, "What difference does it make whether you know [the Way of strategy] or not?" Zhao Kuo[2] [who did not know] lost his kingdom to the state of Qin. Zhang Liang[3] [who did know] helped build the Han kingdom.[4] The difference between knowing and not knowing [the Way of combat strategy] is as obvious as the "fish eye" (that the snake gifted to the Marquis of Sui for saving his life, one of the "Two Treasures of Spring and Autumn"), which does not compare to a real gemstone. Also, a warlord of old[5] once said, "Fighting with a sword is to combat only one enemy at a time [so is not worth my time]. I would rather understand how to destroy thousands of enemies." This is such a narrow-minded remark. Once the Way of swordsmanship is mastered and you take stock, you will see clearly what has to be done to beat the enemy's tactics, whether it be against ten thousand men in pitched battle or in demolishing a well-guarded castle. Good Heavens, who would consider such a thing [as swordsmanship] to be a trivial affair? It is, in fact, a magnificent Way [applicable to the principles of all things].

One who receives sustained instruction in the particulars of the Way of combat strategy will arrive eventually. That is not to say it is easy. If you purge yourself of mistaken ideas and methods in pursuit of the Way, progress in a correct manner, train day in and day out endeavoring to become an expert, a mystical power will aid you in mastery [of the principles of

---

[2] Zhao Kuo (died 260 BCE) was a general of the state of Zhao in ancient China's Warring States period.

[3] Zhang Liang (c. 3rd century BCE–186 BCE) was a general and statesman of the early Western Han dynasty.

[4] Musashi quotes these examples from *Records of the Grand Historian* (*Shiji*), a detailed record of the history of ancient China written around 94 BCE by a Han dynasty official.

[5] Xiang Yu (232–202 BCE) was a powerful warlord of the late Qin dynasty.

strategy]. [What is the "direct path"? (*jikidō*)] Simply by look-ing you will be able to tell what it is and what it is not. If your [daily] deportment is conducted according to the Way, you will not falter even if you do not possess in-depth knowledge. You will not regret your actions. You will eventually become a master [of the Way].

Even someone who has perfected various skills [of the sword], and who can execute techniques expertly, he will fail as if he were scooping broth with his hands when it comes to conveying his knowledge to others.

My Way alone [as it conforms to the principles] is mastered by the spirit so that the body can exhibit the skills. According-ly, one will be a master for eternity. Any successor who talks of a true "Way" is most certainly following mine. Why are there so many different "Ways" when there is but one that is valid? When somebody favors something new in an attempt to break from the old ways, that is, in essence, discarding the level path for the sake of a [pointless] detour.

I say this as Heaven is my witness. Boasting I am not. The Way should be thought of as follows: there is only a sincere heart and a "direct path." This concludes my introduction.

Kumamoto Castle

THE PATH
WALKED ALONE
DOKKŌDŌ

独 行 道

Main Points

* *This document was written by Musashi on the twelfth day of the fifth month, Shōho 2 (1645), one week before he died. It is a reflection on his life.*

* *He is said to have written the 21 one-line articles the day he handed the Gorin-no-sho manuscript to his disciple, Terao Magonojō.*

* *From the middle of the Edo period, this short document was treasured by adherents of Niten Ichi-ryū and became known as the Jiseisho (pledge).*

* *There are other translations of Dokkōdō. Although ambiguous in terms of the original Japanese language, I chose to translate the content as Musashi's self-reflective statements rather than as a formula for others to follow.*

1. I did not infringe upon the Way of successive generations.[1]
2. I sought not pleasure for pleasure's sake.
3. I harbored no biased feelings.
4. I thought lightly of myself and profoundly of the world.
5. I succumbed not to greed for the duration of my life.
6. I held no regrets for past deeds.
7. I was never jealous of others over matters of good and evil.
8. In all things, I never despaired over parting.[2]
9. I never held malice toward others, nor they toward me.
10. I steered clear of the path to attachment.[3]
11. I held no preferences for anything.
12. I cared not where I lived.
13. I sought not the taste of fine food.
14. I possessed no old items of historical consequence to pass on.[4]
15. I adhered not to superstitious beliefs.
16. Apart from weapons, I sought not superfluous trappings.[5]
17. I spurned not death in the Way.[6]
18. I sought not the possession of goods or fiefs for my old age.
19. I respected the deities and Buddha without seeking their aid.
20. I abandoned my body but not my honor.
21. I never drifted from the Way of combat strategy.

---

[1] Musashi is alluding to the idea of universal principles that must always be upheld by humanity.
[2] An allusion to death.
[3] In other words, falling in love.
[4] Family heirlooms and suchlike.
[5] All the warrior needs is a roof over his head and the tools of his trade.
[6] The warrior must never be afraid of dying in the pursuit of his Way.

The Kokura Monument
Kokura-hibun
小倉碑文

(See photo on page 148.)

Main Points

* *This monument was erected by Musashi's adopted son, Miyamoto Iori, in 1654.*

* *It is located close to the site where Musashi dueled with Ganryū Kojirō in 1610.*

* *Because it was erected less than ten years after Musashi's death, it is considered comparatively reliable in terms of its account of his career.*

天仰　實相　圓満　兵法　逝去　不絶
"Ten wa aogu ni, jisshō enman no heihō, seikyo shite taezu"

Looking up at Heaven,
The Combat Strategy of
Ultimate Reality and Harmony
Even in [his] Death
Endures Forever

Monument to the late Shinmen Musashi Genshin Niten, master of swordsmanship beyond compare, descendant of the Akamatsu clan of Harima. He died on the 19th day, 5th month, Shohō 2 [1645], in Kumamoto, province of Higo. On the 19th day, 4th Month, Jōō 3 [1654], this monument was reverently erected by his faithful son [Miyamoto Iori].

Taking one's chances and adjusting to circumstances are characteristic of one who has mastered the Way of a distinguished general. Studying tactics and arduous training in the martial arts are preconditions for men of war. Who was it that walked the dual path of the brush and the sword, whose hands danced in the fray, whose spirited name and honor preceded him? A great man from Harima province, he referred to himself as Musashi Genshin Niten, and was a proud descendant of the Shinmen, a scion of the Akamatsu clan. As I remember, born with a magnanimous spirit, he concerned himself not with trivialities as he was an extraordinary man. He founded the school of swordsmanship which used two swords.

His father's name was Muni, an expert in the *jitte* (truncheon). Musashi followed his father and practiced the martial arts unremittingly day and night while ruminating on the principles of the *jitte*. He learned immeasurable things, recognizing that the humble *jitte* had many unexpected benefits far greater than that of the sword. Nevertheless, the *jitte* is a weapon not often carried. Compared to this, two swords are always worn at the hip. Therefore, utilizing both swords can be just as advantageous as the principle underlying the *jitte*. Musashi gave up the art of the *jitte* in favor of using two swords. His skill with dual swords was as magnificent as a sword dance. His iron swords soared and his wooden swords vaulted. Although his adversaries ran hither and thither to escape his blows, their evasive movements were futile. He seemed like a bolt shot from a powerful crossbow. Never did he miss his mark. Even the great Chinese warrior Yang would have been no match for Musashi. His skill in swordsmanship was sublime and courage emanated from his very being.

Musashi first arrived in the province of Harima when he was thirteen years old. At that tender age, he was keen to test himself in combat against the swordsman Arima Kihei of the Shintō-ryū. It was a comfortable victory for Musashi. When he was sixteen, he ventured to Tajima province in the spring months. It was there that he challenged the formidable swordsman known as Akiyama. Calling for a test of skills, he successfully struck his adversary down without breaking a sweat. His name started surfacing in the region's towns because of these feats of valor.

Musashi then traveled to the capital. It was there, in Kyoto, that the Yoshioka family, veritable masters of the sword, resided. Musashi challenged the family heir, Yoshioka Seijirō, to a match which was to take place at a spot called Rendaino on the edge of the city. There, both men fought courageously like a dragon against a tiger. It was a decisive blow from Musashi's wooden sword that ended the match, snuffing out Yoshioka's breath as he fell to the ground, barely alive. As he had been felled by a single blow, Musashi decided not to end his life. Seijirō's students picked up their limp master and carried him away on a board. After undergoing a course of medical treatment and bathing at hot springs, he recovered but he gave up swordsmanship and became a priest.

Later on, Musashi pitted himself against Yoshioka Denshichirō on the outer periphery of the capital, Kyoto. Denshichirō arrived at the site of the duel with a wooden sword measuring more than five feet [1.5 meters] in length. Undaunted, Musashi tussled with his foe and after wresting his weapon from him, delivered a fatal blow with it. The hapless Yoshioka fell to the ground and died soon after.

Yoshioka disciples schemed revenge, justifying their underhand tactics by saying "It is permissible in strategy to do what needs to be done though it is deemed dishonorable. All armies must concoct plans to prevail in war." They congregated at a place called Sagarimatsu on the outskirts of Kyoto with Yoshioka Matashichirō. He and several hundred of his disciples, with staffs and bows in hand, assembled with the intention of destroying Musashi.

Musashi was astute enough to know what his opponent was planning, and he also knew that an opportunity would present itself to him in spite of their efforts. Seeing through the Yoshioka strategy, he told his own disciples to hang back as the affair was not their concern. "What if hordes of angry men come for your blood?" they cried? "I will observe them passively as if watching the clouds float by in the sky. What have I to fear?" he replied.

When the intrepid Musashi charged head first into the fray, they dispersed in terror as if being hunted by a wild animal. Too frightened to carry on, they left the scene. The people of Kyoto were astonished at Musashi's courage and remarkable strategy that allowed a single man to defeat many foes. What unknown wisdom underpinned his swordsmanship? The Yoshioka clan were teachers of the art of war to noblemen Their reputation preceded them as genuine masters in the art of the sword. Even during the rule of the shogun, Ashikaga Yoshiteru, Muni [Musashi's adoptive father] was summoned to take part in three matches against the Yoshioka school's patriarch in front of the shogun himself. Yoshioka triumphed in one of the bouts, but winning two of the three, Muni was declared "Peerless swordsman of the realm." Musashi had already successfully engaged in several matches against the Yoshioka family during his time in the capital. Through their defeats, the reputation of the mighty house of Yoshika started to decline.

There was another renowned swordsman in the land known as Ganryū. He wanted to challenge Musashi to a duel to settle the issue of who was the better warrior. To this end, he challenged Musashi to a test of mortal combat with swords. Musashi said, "Please use a real sword and savor its merits. I, however, will use a wooden sword to teach you of its higher principles." The contest was arranged.

In the narrow strait between Nagato and Buzen there lies an island known as Funajima. It was here that the contest was to take place, and a time was agreed upon. Ganryū arrived with his sword measuring more than three feet [1 meter] in length. He fought Musashi in mortal combat, but Musashi knocked him dead with a single blow of his wooden sword during a flash of thunder and lightning. Following this momentous duel, the name of the island was changed to Ganyūjima.

Musashi took part in more than sixty duels from the age of thirteen through to thirty. Never once did he fail to win, but he would say that he was only the winner if he was able to hit his adversary between the eyebrows. This was something he maintained his whole life.

There must be thousands, no, tens of thousands of men who have engaged in mortal combat but none can compare to the greatness of Musashi. He is the one and only and his fame has spread far and wide across the four seas. All and sundry know and praise the name. His memory lingers deep in all who understand such matters. He is remembered as a man who was peculiar but extraordinary and in a class of his own. Musashi was truly a man of incredible strength and spirit. He would say that the art of swordsmanship can only be learned by the heart through arduous training. "Once the self has been liberated through training, commanding an army or governing a province is surely not difficult to achieve."

Musashi was already well-known for his skill in swordsmanship when Ishida Jibunoshō, a vassal of the Toyotomi clan, staged his rebellion and when Hideyori's insurgencies were carried out in Osaka and Settsu. But no words can truly describe his greatness and courage. Musashi knew correct etiquette, music, archery, horsemanship, writing, arithmetic and the classics. He was talented in the genteel arts. In fact, there was little he was not gifted in. As he lay on his deathbed in Higo, he wrote, "Looking up at Heaven, the strategy of ultimate reality and harmony, even with my death, will endure forever."

As his devoted son, I hereby place this monument in his honor so that all may know of this great man's life. I sincerely hope that generations of people will read my eulogy to this astonishing man. So great he was!

Erected by Miyamoto Iori

References

Akabane Tatsuo, *Musashi Muhai no Gihō*, BAB Japan, 2019.

All Japan Kendo Federation, *Japanese–English Dictionary of Kendo*, Tokyo: All Japan Kendo Federation, 2011.

Asoshina Yasuo (ed.), *Zusetsu: Miyamoto Musashi no Jitsuzō*, Tokyo: Shin Jinbutsu Ōraisha, 2003.

Bennett, Alexander C., *Kendo:, Culture of the Sword*, Berkeley: University of California Press, 2015.

Blakney, Charles P. (trans.), *The Book of Five Rings*, New York: Bantam Books, 1994.

de Lange, William (trans. and ed.), *The Real Musashi: Origins of a Legend— The Bushū Denraiki*, Warren, CT: Floating World Editions, 2010.

_____ (trans. and ed.), *The Real Musashi: Origins of a Legend II—The Bukōden*, Warren, CT: Floating World Editions, 2011.

_____ *The Real Musashi: A Miscellany* (*Origins of a Legend III*), Warren, CT: Floating World Editions, 2016.

Fukuda Masahide, *Miyamoto Musashi: Kenkyū Ronbunshū*, Rekiken, 2003.

Groff, David K. (trans.), *The Five Rings: Miyamoto Musashi's Art of Strategy*, London: Watkins Publishing, 2012.

Harris, Victor (trans.), *The Book of Five Rings*, Woodstock, NY: The Overlook Press, 1974.

Hayakawa Junzaburō (ed.), *Bujutsu Sōsho*, Tokyo: Hachiman Shoten, 2003.

Imai Masayuki, *Dokkōdō: Niten-Ichi-ryū Seihō*, Oita, Japan: M. Imai, 1995.

Imamura Yoshio, *Nihon Budō Taikei*, Kyoto: Dōhōsha, 1982.

Inagaki Hisao, *A Dictionary of Japanese Buddhist Terms*, Kyoto: Nagata Bunshodō, 1984.

Issai Chozan (trans. William Scott Wilson), *The Demon's Sermon on the Martial Arts: And Other Tales*, Tokyo: Kodansha International, 2006.

Iwamoto Yutaka, *Nihon Bukkyōgo Jiten*, Tokyo: Heibon-sha, 1988.

Kaku Kōzo, *Miyamoto Musashi Jiten*, Tokyo: Tokyo-dō, 2001.

Kamata Shigeo, *Gorin-no-sho*, Tokyo: Kōdansha, 1986.

Kamiko Tadashi, *Gorin-no-sho*, Tokyo: Tokuma Shoten, 1963.

Maruoka Muneo (ed.), *Miyamoto Musashi Meihin Shūsei*, Tokyo: Kodansha, 1984.

Miyamoto Musashi Iseki Kenshōkai, *Miyamoto Musashi*, Tokyo: Miyamoto Musashi Iseki Kenshōkai, 1909.

Morita Sakae, *Teisetsu no Ayamari wo Tadasu Miyamoto Musashi Seiden*, Taiiku to Sports-sha, 2014.

Nakamura Hajime, *Bukkyōgo Daijiten*, Tokyo: Shoseki, 1981.

Okada Kazuo, *Miyamoto Musashi no Subete*, Tokyo: Shin Jinbutsu Ōrai-sha, 1992.

Okouchi Shōji, *Gorin-no-sho*, Tokyo: Kyōikusha, 1980.

Ōmori Sōgen, *Miyamoto Musashi Hitsu: Dokkōdō*, Tokyo: Kōdansha, 1974.

Ōura Tatsuo, *Gorin-no-sho to Niten-Ichi-ryū no Gokui*, Tokyo: Management-sha Publishing, 1989.

Rogers, John M., "Arts of War in Times of Peace: Swordsmanship in the Honchō Bugei Shōden," Chapter 6, *Monumenta Nipponica*, 46 (2), 1991, pp. 173–202.

Sasamori Junzō, *Ittō-ryū Gokui*, Tokyo: Taiiku to Sports-sha, 1986.

Takano Sasaburō, *Kendō*, Tokyo: Shimazu Shobō, 1913.

Takuan Sōhō (trans. William Scott Wilson), *The Unfettered Mind: Writings of the Zen Master to the Sword Master*, Tokyo: Kodansha International, 1986.

Taniguchi Motome, *Kanjin, Miyamoto Musashi Genshin*, Tokyo: Buōsha, 1999.

Tokitsu Kenji (trans. Sherab Chädzin Kohn), *Miyamoto Musashi: His Life and Writings*, London: Shambhala Publications, 2004.

Uozumi Takashi, *Miyamoto Musashi: "Heihō no Michi" wo Ikiru*, Tokyo: Iwanami Shoten, 2008.

_____, *Miyamoto Musashi: Nihonjin no michi*, Tokyo: Perikansha, 2002.

_____, "Research of Miyamoto Musashi's *Gorin-no-sho*," in *Budo Studies: An Anthology of Research into Budo in the 21st Century*, Katsuura: Institute of Budo Studies, 2000, pp. 1–37.

_____, "Research of Miyamoto Musashi's *Gorin-no-sho*: From the Perspective of Japanese Intellectual History," in Alexander Bennett (ed.), *Budo Perspectives*, Vol. 1, Auckland, NZ: Kendo World Publications, Ltd, 2005, pp. 45–67.

_____, *Teihon: Gorin-no-sho*, Tokyo: Shin Jinbutsu Ōraisha, 2005.

Watanabe Ichirō, *Gorin-no-sho*, Tokyo: Iwanami Shoten, 1985.

Watatani *Musashi Matabee: Kyōdo no Kengō-tachi*, Nojigiku Bunko, 1963.

Wilson, William Scott, *The Lone Samurai: The Life of Miyamoto Musashi*, Tokyo: Kodansha International, 2004.

Wilson, William Scott (trans.), *The Book of Five Rings*, Tokyo: Kodansha International, 2001.

Yagyū Munenori (trans. William Scott Wilson), *The Life-Giving Sword: Secret Teachings from the House of the Shogun*, Tokyo: Kodansha International, 2003..

"Books to Span the East and West"

Tuttle Publishing was founded in 1832 in the small New England town of Rutland, Vermont [USA]. Our core values remain as strong today as they were then—to publish best-in-class books which bring people together one page at a time. In 1948, we established a publishing outpost in Japan—and Tuttle is now a leader in publishing English-language books about the arts, languages and cultures of Asia. The world has become a much smaller place today and Asia's economic and cultural influence has grown. Yet the need for meaningful dialogue and information about this diverse region has never been greater. Over the past seven decades, Tuttle has published thousands of books on subjects ranging from martial arts and paper crafts to language learning and literature—and our talented authors, illustrators, designers and photographers have won many prestigious awards. We welcome you to explore the wealth of information available on Asia at www.tuttlepublishing.com.

First published by Tuttle Publishing, an imprint of Periplus Editions (HK) Ltd.

www.tuttlepublishing.com

This Paperback Edition Copyright © 2020 Alexander Bennett

Library of Congress Control Number: 2018949133

ISBN: 978-4-8053-1616-0

27 26 25 24   8 7 6 5 4   2401TP
Printed in Singapore

TUTTLE PUBLISHING® is a registered trademark of Tuttle Publishing, a division of Periplus Editions (HK) Ltd.

Distributed by

North America, Latin America & Europe
Tuttle Publishing
364 Innovation Drive, North Clarendon
VT 05759-9436 U.S.A.
Tel: 1 (802) 773-8930
Fax: 1 (802) 773-6993
info@tuttlepublishing.com
www.tuttlepublishing.com

Japan
Tuttle Publishing
Yaekari Building 3rd Floor 5-4-12 Osaki
Shinagawa-ku, Tokyo 141 0032
Tel: (81) 3 5437-0171
Fax: (81) 3 5437-0755
sales@tuttle.co.jp
www.tuttle.co.jp

Asia Pacific
Berkeley Books Pte. Ltd.
3 Kallang Sector #04-01
Singapore 349278
Tel: (65) 6741-2178
Fax: (65) 6741-2179
inquiries@periplus.com.sg
www.tuttlepublishing.com